HBR Guide to
Buying a Small Business

Harvard Business Review Guides

Arm yourself with the advice you need to succeed on the job, from the most trusted brand in business. Packed with how-to essentials from leading experts, the HBR Guides provide smart answers to your most pressing work challenges.

The titles include:

HBR Guide to Better Business Writing

HBR Guide to Building Your Business Case

HBR Guide to Buying a Small Business

HBR Guide to Coaching Employees

HBR Guide to Data Analytics Basics for Managers

HBR Guide to Finance Basics for Managers

HBR Guide to Getting the Mentoring You Need

HBR Guide to Getting the Right Job

HBR Guide to Getting the Right Work Done

HBR Guide to Giving Effective Feedback

HBR Guide to Leading Teams

HBR Guide to Making Every Meeting Matter

HBR Guide to Managing Stress at Work

HBR Guide to Managing Up and Across

HBR Guide to Negotiating

HBR Guide to Networking

HBR Guide to Office Politics

HBR Guide to Persuasive Presentations

HBR Guide to Project Management

HBR Guide to
Buying a Small Business

Richard S. Ruback
Royce Yudkoff

HARVARD BUSINESS REVIEW PRESS

Boston, Massachusetts

Copyright 2017 Harvard Business School Publishing Corporation

All rights reserved

Printed in the United States of America

10 9 8 7 6 5 4 3

No part of this publication may be reproduced, stored in or introduced into a retrieval system, or transmitted, in any form, or by any means (electronic, mechanical, photocopying, recording, or otherwise), without the prior permission of the publisher. Requests for permission should be directed to permissions@hbsp.harvard.edu, or mailed to Permissions, Harvard Business School Publishing, 60 Harvard Way, Boston, Massachusetts 02163.

The web addresses referenced in this book were live and correct at the time of the book's publication but may be subject to change.

Library of Congress data is forthcoming

ISBN: 978-1-63369-250-3
eISBN:978-1-63369-251-0

The paper used in this publication meets the requirements of the American National Standard for Permanence of Paper for Publications and Documents in Libraries and Archives Z39.48–1992.

Contents

Contents

Contents

Preface

This book takes a big idea from our popular courses at the Harvard Business School and for the first time shares it beyond campus. The big idea is that you can buy an existing small business, right now, and run it as a CEO. Each year, we teach hundreds of MBA students about this kind of entrepreneurship, and dozens of them follow this path immediately after graduation.

About five years ago, we developed a course on small businesses to fill what we saw as a gap in the school's offerings. We chose to study small businesses because it allowed us to apply our skills and experience to a vital segment of the economy that we believe should get more attention—especially from entrepreneurially minded men and women who can become owners and managers of these companies.

We became even more fascinated with smaller businesses the more we learned about them. Our students became engrossed as well; last year, every seat in the courses we offered was filled. And the number of students who go on to buy a small business directly after graduation continues to rapidly grow each year. We are not surprised: These businesses give our students the opportunity to be leaders early in their careers, to apply their common sense and their general management expertise, and to fashion a work environment that meets their goals.

While our primary interest in small businesses is in teaching and research, we have also become investors in some of the businesses our former students have acquired, including some of those described in this book. We've put our money into these opportunities because we are enthusiastic and confident about the potential of entrepreneurship through acquisition and because we've been excited to see so many individuals succeed—on so many levels—when they decide to follow this challenging, often tortuous, often fun, and always exciting path.

As we've seen the demand for our course increase, we wrote this book to bring the idea to a wider audience, beyond the walls of our classroom, and to guide you through the process of buying a small business. We hope that many of you find the idea as compelling as our students do—and as we ourselves do—and that you find success in pursuing one of the many unique opportunities available in this little-known market.

PART ONE

Think Big, Buy Small

This part of the book introduces you to the opportunity to become an owner and a CEO of a successful existing business. In **chapter 1, "The Opportunity: Entrepreneurship Through Acquisition,"** we describe the opportunity involved in acquiring a small business, the magnitude of such an opportunity, and the practicality of achieving it. You'll also meet people who have traveled this path, and you can begin to think about whether you want to do what they did. **Chapter 2, "Is Entrepreneurship Through Acquisition for You?,"** then focuses on the skills and traits we've repeatedly seen in successful, satisfied entrepreneurs through acquisition. Whether this path is right for you depends on what you value, what you don't, and what skills you can draw on. Finally, in **chapter 3, "The Acquisition Process,"** we give you an overview of what to expect when you are searching for and purchasing a smaller business—steps that we will revisit in more detail in the remaining parts of this book.

CHAPTER 1

The Opportunity: Entrepreneurship Through Acquisition

If you are a manager thinking about making a change in your career or a newly minted MBA looking to begin a management career, this is an opportunity you should consider: You can buy an existing business, right now, and run it as CEO. We call this *entrepreneurship through acquisition,* and through our work teaching and researching the subject at Harvard Business School, we have seen many professionals find it an intriguing and rewarding alternative to a more traditional job.

Running your own company offers a radically different career path and career lifestyle than does working at a traditional large corporation. It allows you to lead an organization, make decisions that matter, and have the flexibility to work in a way that suits you best. If you have struggled to find professional independence and fulfillment in bigger companies, entrepreneurship through acquisition could be a path for you.

The financial prospects of buying and running a small business are also appealing. Entrepreneurs through acquisition usually purchase their company using a combination of debt from banks and equity from investors and structure the purchase so that they retain a meaningful economic stake in the business. Such a stake means that you have the opportunity for significant financial reward. You can buy high-quality small businesses for a price that allows you and your investors to earn an excellent return on your investment. Some of this return will be cash flows that you'll distribute each year to your investors. Eventually, you and your investors might sell the business, and if you've been able to grow it, you should be able to sell it for far more than the purchase price, resulting in a meaningful financial gain. So, entrepreneurship through acquisition offers both an exciting career and a significant investment opportunity.

Part of what ignites our passion for small businesses is also the variety and uniqueness of the businesses themselves. Entrepreneurs whom we've studied have gone into home health care, exotic travel, musical instrument rental, specialized software, and manufacturing. Some of these businesses provide services you might have known about, like commercial window washing for skyscrapers; others you may never have thought of, like testing fire hoses. These are smaller firms with steady annual revenues of $5.0 million to $15.0 million and annual cash flows of $750,000 to $3.0 million. They aren't rapidly evolving tech companies or glamorous businesses, and journalists don't write as much about entrepreneurs through acquisition as they do about founders of big start-ups. But we estimate that there are about 200,000 of these businesses in the United States—with many more around the world—and that every year thousands of them are bought and sold.[1]

You may be more qualified to run a small business than you think. Experiences such as managing others and taking on responsibility for financial performance give you much of the background you need. We'll introduce you to a number of entrepreneurs through acquisition—people we've known and worked with (and in some cases even invested in) so you can learn from their experiences. You may see that these people are not so different from you. (See, for example, the sidebar "Tony Bautista: Entrepreneur Through Acquisition.") Almost none of them were CEOs before; rather, they typically have 5 to 15 years of professional experience, mostly at the junior level, and some have middle-management experience. None had bought a business before or had significant personal wealth when they started, and all of them raised money from investors to complete their acquisition. Some of the entrepreneurs pursued opportunities in the United States; others found that this path was the perfect way to put their management skills to work in their home countries around the world. And contrary to popular myths about entrepreneurs, all of them are generally careful people rather than reckless risk takers.

Instead, what sets them apart is that they are energetic, tenacious, and smart individuals open to pursuing opportunities in smaller businesses and niche industries rather than focusing only on opportunities with the biggest brands or in the most popular sectors.

Tenacity is important because there can be some significant challenges along the way. As we studied the market for these businesses, we were surprised to find that the earliest stumbling block for purchasers—and one of the biggest—comes in the search for and acquisition of the business. We've seen potential buyers quit because their search has dragged on unproductively too long; we've seen deals fall through after months of work because the buyer didn't ask the right questions of the seller at the beginning of the process; and we've seen

---

TONY BAUTISTA:
ENTREPRENEUR THROUGH ACQUISITION

Tony Bautista, CEO of Fail Safe LLC, a leading fire-hose testing service for local fire departments, acquired the company after a 10-month search. "Looking back," Tony observed, "the biggest barrier wasn't capital, wasn't experience, wasn't contacts. More than anything, the barrier is internal: It's making the decision to do it."

Boston-born Bautista grew up with his younger sister in a household headed by a single mother, herself a first-generation immigrant to the United States. "We

---

TONY BAUTISTA:
ENTREPRENEUR THROUGH ACQUISITION

were certainly never hungry," he reflected, "but mom usually worked two jobs, and we also relied on food stamps. More than anything, my mother impressed on my sister and me the value of an education." Tony was enrolled in a weekend and after-school acceleration program at his local public school, and the program eventually led to a full scholarship to college. While there, he earned money managing a tutoring service for high school students.

After college, Tony worked for a large investment-management company for over three years. "I learned a lot about financial analysis and accounting," he said, "but I felt I was just shuffling numbers around. When I ran the tutoring service, I could see the impact of my work. This disconnect bothered me, and when my mom passed away prematurely in 2010, I was galvanized to do something about it." Tony enrolled in business school and worked in venture capital in the summer between his first and second years. "That didn't do it for me either," Bautista reflected. "Venture capital still seemed removed from what had satisfied me so much in the tutoring firm—satisfying clients, giving a paycheck to employees, and directly building a business. On top of that, backing start-ups seemed so risky to me."

During his second year at business school, Tony decided to search for an existing smaller business to

(*continued*)

TONY BAUTISTA:
ENTREPRENEUR THROUGH ACQUISITION

(*continued*)

buy, although he was only 28 years old. "Besides being a hard worker," he said, "I think my greatest strength is being able to relate to a wide range of people. Not coming from a wealthy background but going to college and business school taught me this. I could talk to business brokers about numbers and financing a purchase; I could talk to rough-edged owners who ran firms with lots of blue-collar employees; I could talk to investors who might back me in my purchase."

In 2014, Tony acquired Fail Safe from its retiring CEO/owner. Fail Safe sends crews to local firehouses to perform annual safety testing of fire hoses; Tony is immersed in the tasks of talking to customers, scheduling, managing his crew chiefs, and the other myriad tasks of running a mission-critical service business with workers spread across many states. "Looking back," he said, "my biggest gap was a lack of experience in the details of operating a business: How exactly do you run a monthly payroll? for example. I learned as I went; it was sometimes painful, but not fatal."

Bautista added: "For me, the most satisfying experience is having employees do work for which I send them a paycheck: I am supporting someone who is like me, and, of course, when I'm doing this, it also means my company is making money."

starry-eyed searchers buy businesses that didn't live up to expectations. We've also seen many people who didn't even start the process, because they didn't feel qualified or didn't know how to begin their search or raise the capital to pay for their search or their acquisition.

The search process is critical. If it works, you'll be managing the business for a significant number of years—perhaps much of your remaining working life. The financial success of the business will determine your lifestyle, your location, and even the schools you can send your kids to during that time and after. There is also no easy out if you make a mistake and buy the wrong company. If your company fails, you'll likely lose it and all of your savings, as well as any investments you've accepted from friends and family. Choosing well is very important.

In this book, we give you the advice and tools you need to successfully find and purchase the right small business for you to run. We'll show you how to take several important steps:

- Determine if this path is right for you.

- Use your time and resources during the search efficiently.

- Pick the right business for you.

- Ensure that the owner is serious about selling at a reasonable market price.

- Raise the capital you need for your search and for buying the business you have selected.

- Focus on the right priorities as you close the deal—and beyond.

Managing the Risks of Ownership

Does running a small business seem risky? Perhaps you're imagining the things that could go wrong once you acquire a company: What if it stops generating as much revenue when you are at its helm? What if your most valued customers switch to a competitor? What if the market for the hot new technology you've invested in crashes? What if you can't pay the employees who depend on you? What if, what if, what if? You can probably assemble a nearly endless list of challenges. It's true; a lot of bad things could happen. Be mindful that they could happen to a big firm too but, as a small firm, your enterprise is certainly less sturdy than a large corporation.

But during your purchase process, there are ways to mitigate these risks. In this book, we show you how to find a business that is *enduringly profitable,* one that is more likely to continue to have a stable income over time. It's not always easy to know what makes a small business enduringly profitable, but we have identified a few indicators to use as you evaluate potential businesses: for example, the business should be an established one that is growing slowly and has recurring customers. We recommend against buying a tech company or any business in a volatile industry, and we urge you to stay away from companies that "just" need a turnaround. We think "dull" businesses are terrific business opportunities— and a great way to mitigate the risk of small-business ownership.

Also, recognize that the alternatives to entrepreneurship through acquisition may actually be more risky than you think. If you're considering entrepreneurship by start-up, for example, you must build a company from scratch, without knowing whether the product or service can support a profitable business. When you start a company—before you make any money—you face a long list of required tasks. You must develop a product or service, identify your potential customers, and figure out how to deliver the offering to the customers. You must also hire all your workers, market to customers, build a management system, and then hope your offering is something customers want to buy at a price high enough for you to make a profit. Buying an existing, enduringly profitable business is less risky—not 100% safe, but much safer because the fundamental questions about the viability of the basic business model have already been answered. When you buy a business, the product or service is already established, and if you buy the kind of company we recommend, it is likely to produce steady cash flows while you focus on improvements and growth.

And what about working at a large firm? All of the entrepreneurs we studied turned down or quit a good job at a large organization to pursue this opportunity. When we asked them about the risks involved, they reminded us that working in a large company is also risky. Coca-Cola, Intel, or Tata are not going to vanish the way that a small enterprise might, but in a large company, your division might shut down, your job might be eliminated as part of a reduction in force, or your career could be held back because of the politicking common to large organizations. Also, as you become more senior in a bigger business, your role often shifts, perhaps to one you enjoy less or in which you are less likely to excel. Often, these risks are not apparent until it's too late to do anything about them—and as a single employee, you have very little control over the situation. Small-firm entrepreneur Charles Muszynski, co-owner and co-CEO of outsourced waste services firm Talismark, likes to say, "I like being the only person who can fire me."

To be sure, the entrepreneurship-through-acquisition path is not an easy one. It requires much hard work, the ability to bounce back from disappointments, common sense, and business acumen. Though you face less uncertainty than you would in founding your own start-up, there is still risk—especially in the search itself. And you'll have to do without certain comforts, such as a familiar peer group at work. But many of the entrepreneurs we studied found that what they've gotten out of the experience far outweighs the costs.

Reaping the Rewards: The Financial Opportunity

Beyond the salary that you pay yourself—which may admittedly be more modest than what you might earn in a senior position at a large organization—your business is an investment in which you have a meaningful economic stake. The purchase price of smaller businesses tends to be relatively low compared with their profits, making them appealing as investments.

Consider this representative example. One of our former students recently bought a business for $10.25

million. The business generates a yearly pretax operating profit of $2.5 million. That means he and his investors are earning almost a 25% annual return on this $10.25 million purchase. If that same $10.25 million were invested in a traditional investment vehicle—like a well-diversified mutual fund—it would earn far less, perhaps less than 10%, or $1.0 million.

Of course, this entrepreneur didn't see this entire return. The total acquisition cost included $250,000 of closing costs. He funded the acquisition by borrowing $7.5 million and raising $3.0 million of equity from a group of investors. So his deal to purchase the company looked like this:

Borrowed	$7.5 million
+ Raised from investors	$3.0 million
Total cost	$10.5 million

The interest on the $7.5 million of debt was 6.5%, or about $490,000 per year, leaving about $2.0 million per year available to the owners (the buyer and the investors):

Pretax operating income	$2.5 million
− Interest expense	($490,000)
Cash available for owners	$2.01 million

Per his deal with his investors, our entrepreneur received 20% of any profit from running (or eventually selling) the company, in addition to an annual starting salary of $150,000 to run the business. So, in the first year after acquisition, his financials looked like this:

Share owned by entrepreneur (20% × $2.0 million)	$400,000
+ Salary	$150,000
Entrepreneur's year one wealth creation	$550,000

Of course, only the $150,000 was in cash; the rest of the compensation is deferred and contingent on the outcome of the investment. And all of these are before taxes. But this is still an impressive increase in our entrepreneur's anticipated wealth in a short time.

Furthermore, the entrepreneur bought the business because he plans to grow it, increasing not only its annual profits but also its total value. For example, if he runs it for 10 years and is able to grow it at 5% a year, his annual wealth creation would be about $850,000. And while the majority of his return on his investment comes from the ongoing profits from the business, if he were to sell the company and if market conditions were the same as when he bought it, his share of the gain on the sale would be roughly $1.3 million. In total, adding up all of his compensation over the 10 years, plus his share of the gain on exit, he would pocket over $8.0 million before taxes.

At the heart of these remarkable rewards is the fact that these businesses are often available at prices that are low relative to the companies' annual profits. Opportunities like this exist because most owners of successful smaller firms eventually *need* to sell them—to retire or because of health issues, divorce, acrimony among business partners, or other factors. Their children may have completely different professions—their daughter a doctor, their son a poet—and no one in the family is interested in taking over a manufacturing business. Owners of bigger businesses have more options, but owners of smaller companies typically need to find someone outside their firm who can both buy their company and take over its management.

But few people have both the ability to raise the required capital and the interest in managing a small company. And the difficulty of finding enduringly profitable acquisition targets means that potential buyers who have the ability to finance and then manage a small company will also need to find the right company first. The search requires significant time, effort, and funding. So, while there is a steady supply of small-business owners who are compelled to sell, there are few buyers. This disparity keeps the prices of smaller companies attractive to buyers.

Beyond the potential financial rewards, buying a business can also give you professional independence and personal fulfillment. In most larger businesses, it is difficult for people to obtain meaningful leadership responsibility early in their careers. But when you're the CEO of a small business, you set the strategy of the firm and make every significant decision about how the firm is run. For some people, like Greg Ambrosia, one of the most attractive elements of buying a small company is that it provides the opportunity to have an immediate impact on his company and its employees (see the sidebar "Greg Ambrosia: Entrepreneur Through Acquisition").

GREG AMBROSIA:
ENTREPRENEUR THROUGH ACQUISITION

On winter mornings, it's chilly inside the cavernous staging room at Citywide Building Services. Citywide is the leading high-rise window cleaner in the Dallas/Fort Worth Metroplex. At 6:15 one morning, 48 washers watch CEO Greg Ambrosia as he calls out assignments, and crews begin peeling off in company trucks to make their way across the just-awakening city.

Citywide was founded 30 years earlier by two energetic, entrepreneurial sisters who built the company's preeminent reputation for safety and quality service. The company serves most of the region's tall office, hospital, and university buildings with this essential, quietly recurring service. In 2014, the two founders decided to retire, and Greg acquired the company after about 11 months of searching.

"Being a CEO involves making decisions all the time and successfully working through others," Greg said, "and as a result, this work is completely engaging for me."

Greg didn't come from a business background at all. He grew up in Knoxville, Tennessee, where his father is an orthopedic surgeon, his mother a homemaker, his brother also a surgeon, and his sister a nurse. "I didn't grow up at a dinner table hearing the language of business," he observed. Graduating from high school, he decided not to follow a path into medicine—or into business—but instead was accepted to the U.S. Military

GREG AMBROSIA:
ENTREPRENEUR THROUGH ACQUISITION

Academy at West Point. "In studying high school American history," he said, "I was struck by how many leaders went to West Point. I came to admire the school's tradition and mission of training leaders for service." After graduation, Greg served in Afghanistan, where, among other assignments, he led a company of 120 soldiers in combat and was awarded a Silver Star.

In 2011 he left the army and attended business school to facilitate his transition to civilian life. "I had never held a serious private-sector job. As a result, I didn't know much about accounting, finance, sales management, or other critical business functions. Getting some training in these subjects was necessary for me."

Between his first and second years of business school, Greg interned at a large corporation. "I liked the people and thought they were really smart. But the lack of personal responsibility and authority was just not satisfying for me. That's when I started to consider other paths. I was really looking for an opportunity to show greater leadership and to be entrusted with meaningful responsibility."

Everyone who begins this journey of entrepreneurship through acquisition starts out with different strengths and weaknesses. "My weaknesses were apparent and immediate," he said. "I had never bought

(continued)

**GREG AMBROSIA:
ENTREPRENEUR THROUGH ACQUISITION**

(*continued*)

or financed anything bigger than a car. But I addressed that by teaming up with some investors who could advise me. In contrast, I did have useful experience in leadership, which has translated well to my new role."

After a management transition period with the sellers, Greg has been making decisions that he believes will move Citywide to the next level: recruiting new high-rise washers, upgrading the company's training and safety program, revamping compensation to better align the workers and the company, calling on prospective customers, upgrading Citywide's IT system, and more.

"If there are two things I love most about this job," Greg told us, "it's the being able to affect the outcome of my business and my career, and the ability to help people in my company become more successful at what they do."

Making the Choice

As you decide what you want to do with your career, we hope that you come to see entrepreneurship through acquisition as we do—as an attractive third path, an exciting alternative to big corporations and risky start-ups.

One caveat: Most of the examples of entrepreneurs whom you'll meet in this book are men, and that's because most of the people who have chosen this career path have been men. Nevertheless, we think owning a small business is a great career for women, and we know women who have had great success following that path. All of the financial and lifestyle advantages of owning a small business are available for both men and women, and some of those benefits might be especially valuable to women. No customer, for example, ever imagines paying less for a product or service because the business is owned by a woman. Plus, as much as men value the flexibility of being their own boss, we think women might value it even more, especially if they have primary childcare responsibilities. Robin Kovitz, president at Baskits, Inc., for example, left a successful career in private equity to search for a small business to buy, because she believed it would enable her to spend more time with her young family.

We often wonder why so few women decide to become entrepreneurs through acquisition early in their careers. One explanation, perhaps, is that more-traditional career paths are more attractive for women as those organizations try to correct a historical imbalance. Alternatively, women may more highly value aspects of a more traditional career—such as affiliation—that come with employment by a well-known, prestigious company. Still, some women do search for a small business to acquire early in their careers. Jenn Braus, for example, finished a business school degree, spent much of the next year with her husband volunteering at an orphanage in Central America, and then returned to the United States, where she began searching for a small business to acquire and then run. She acquired Systems Design West, a successful software and services company serving the emergency medical services industry, and is now its CEO.

We also find that some women may view the entrepreneur-through-acquisition path as more appealing later in their careers. We see these women begin to search after having successfully worked in larger organizations while raising families. They decide to turn to entrepreneurship through acquisition because it fits with their evolving interests and lifestyles.

Next Steps

We think the decision to pursue entrepreneurship through acquisition depends on your skills and goals, not your age or gender. In the next chapter, we'll explore more of what makes a good entrepreneur through acquisition to help you decide whether this is the right opportunity for you.

NOTE

1. Our best data on the number of smaller firms in this size range suggest that there are 130,000 to 240,000 such companies, with S+P Capital IQ estimating the lower end and the U.S. Census computing the higher end. If businesses with average revenues of less than $5.0 million are included, the number rises to over 1.4 million.

CHAPTER 2

Is Entrepreneurship Through Acquisition for You?

Is buying a small business right for you? We think that entrepreneurship through acquisition is an extraordinary professional opportunity—but it's not for everyone. While it can yield professional achievement, independence, and financial success, it also takes time, energy, and sacrifice. You'll also need a bit of common sense and business acumen. To decide, you should understand the challenges and the rewards that come with this career and what the everyday work is like.

You don't need to have owned a company before to follow this path successfully; most of the entrepreneurs we've studied were first-time business owners. And you don't need to be personally wealthy, because you'll raise money from investors to fund your acquisition. But the career path needs to be a good fit for you. While successful entrepreneurs are certainly not all alike, there are values, goals, and skills that we've seen repeatedly in people who find great fulfillment in owning their own businesses. Whether this path is right for you depends on your values as well as your skills.

What You Value

There are a number of values that many of us embrace—but for potential entrepreneurs through acquisition, the question is how much you value them, and how much you are willing to give up to maintain a professional lifestyle that puts these first.

Independence

Owners of the kinds of small businesses we study love the flexibility and freedom that come from running their own business. They make decisions themselves, without having to request approval from their bosses. Want to replace a salesperson with someone you think has more energy and drive? Do it. Want to see your daughter's afternoon soccer game? Just go. Your customers care that your product quality is excellent and that your prices are competitive; they don't care how you did it or that you left early last Thursday. We know of people who decided to become business owners because they could run their businesses successfully while still having the flexibility to raise a family, to race cars professionally, or to teach in a religious school. Running an established smaller company usually means long hours, but often there is more control over when those hours occur. Plus, because you choose the company you purchase, you eliminate the companies where the required commitment of the owner doesn't match your lifestyle needs.

Of course, most people would say that they value professional independence—who doesn't like that kind of freedom in the abstract? In truth, however, people often enjoy the structure that larger organizations and bosses can bring. You're told explicitly what to do and, often, how to do it. "Do A, then B, then C"; "hit these sales targets"; "meet this deadline"; "be in the office these hours." It simplifies your professional life: You know what to do, and when it's done, you can go home with little concern over what else you should have done. The structure defines the steps to success. Structure may feel limiting, but independence also brings its own stresses and responsibilities.

When you are your own boss in a smaller, nimble enterprise, you will need to be constantly reevaluating and adjusting your own goals, priorities, and processes yourself. Figuring out *what* to do is always at the very top of your to-do list. And though you don't have a boss, you'll still answer to lenders, investors, customers, suppliers, employees, regulators, and competitors. When something goes wrong, nobody will feel the pain more than you will. You'll wonder what you could have done better. And when you go home at night, you'll be focused on what you should have done that you didn't do and what your priorities should be for tomorrow. It is all up to you.

The challenges of independence begin as you search for a company to buy. Each morning during your search, you will be confronted with a score of activities you could pursue: checking in with brokers, cold-calling owners, reviewing information on companies that are for sale, writing offer letters—the list goes on and on. There is no one to turn to and say, "What's really important? What should I work on next?" It's just you. The ability to organize yourself and focus on what is important is critical to success. So, as you consider whether the day-to-day work of this path is what you are looking for, measure your desire for independence against the challenges that come with it.

Being rewarded for what you do

One of the unique experiences of entrepreneurship—whether it comes from starting your own company or buying one—is that everything you do benefits you and your investors. Make a sale? That's profit for you and your investors. Negotiate a lower rate on insurance coverage or delivery services? The savings belongs to you and your investors. These direct rewards can be a much more powerful motivator than praise from your boss or other organizational rewards. The high level of energy they generate for you both gets things done and sets the pace for the organization.

Direct rewards, of course, work both ways. You can end a month better off than when it began—or worse off. Most searchers and entrepreneurs report that their work involves much greater emotional oscillations—bigger ups and downs—than they had ever experienced working for others. We think this is because the direct rewards, together with being the ultimate decision maker, are an emotionally powerful combination. The good days are truly exhilarating because your work has improved the well-being of those who believe in you and depend on you—like your family and your investors. But when things go badly, it can be really depressing because you have made those you care about worse off. Entrepreneur Greg Ambrosia observed, "My job is exhilarating, but it's also stressful; I feel very responsible to my customers, my employees, and my investors, and of course, I want the company to achieve my goals too. My friends are sometimes surprised when I tell them I experience more stress now than I did leading soldiers in combat. I think that's because in combat, you had short periods of extreme stress followed by long periods without much. As CEO, that feeling of responsibility to get it right doesn't stop."

Ask yourself, Can I calmly work through these inevitable cycles? Can I learn from my mistakes and move on? Can I retain more joy from the ups than misery from the downs? To be successful, you'll need to keep working through these emotional swings. If doing so doesn't match your personality, then entrepreneurship through acquisition probably isn't a good career choice for you.

Learning

Throughout your search, you'll be continuously learning about new businesses and industries, including many that you didn't even know existed. Because great small companies tend to be found in specialized niches of the economy, it's unlikely that you'll know much about the business until you start to investigate it. Once you buy a business, you'll need to immerse yourself in it and quickly become an expert in its critical aspects while knowing at least a bit about all its functions, from marketing and production to legal and accounting.

Learning can be hard. You must be willing to make mistakes as you test your emerging understanding—even if the mistakes cost you your own time and money. You will also need to constantly base decisions on incomplete information because you simply don't have the time to track down all the details or because the information normally available in a larger organization is absent. You'll need to learn to approach problems intuitively and refine that intuition every day as you gain experience. You'll learn that good decisions made quickly are often better than great decisions made slowly. If you are curious and intrigued by business and humble enough to recognize where you need to grow, you'll love this challenge. If not, you'll be miserable.

What You'll Need to Do Without

We've seen that even the best sides of entrepreneurship through acquisition can bring with them some challenges. Indeed, entrepreneurs—and those actively searching for a small business to buy—give up many things you might presently enjoy if you have a job at a large organization. Let's look at some of the most painful to give up— those to which you might be most accustomed.

A regular salary plus benefits

Once you purchase your small business, you and your investors will agree on your salary and what benefits you and your employees enjoy. But searching—yes, just searching—for a company to buy requires a full commitment of all your professional time (we'll address this when we discuss the costs of the search). It isn't something you can successfully do on nights and weekends, like restoring an old car or refinishing your basement. That means you'll have to do without the salary and benefits from a job. What you'll live on depends, in part, on how you finance your search. If you pay for it yourself, you'll be living on your savings or the earnings of your spouse. If you raise money from investors, you'll get some salary and benefits: typically around $80,000 in annual salary while you are searching. It's enough to live on, but it gives you a strong incentive to find the right company to acquire as quickly as possible.

Working for a big brand

It can feel great to have a sense of membership in a large, quality organization that is widely recognized. You're proud of the identity that you get from saying, "I'm with Google," or General Electric, or Coca-Cola.

Though, as entrepreneur Greg Mazur reminds us, owning your own business comes with its own kind of recognition. He told us that when he says, "I'm the CEO and owner of Great Eastern Premium Pet Foods," he takes pride in being the CEO and owner of his own firm.

A community of colleagues

Who do you have lunch with every day? Going to work is partly a social experience, and, in large organizations, you will often find other people who share your values, skills, and educational experiences. These colleagues become your community; they are the people you ski and golf with on weekends and the people you might see socially. In small firms, however, it's hard to come by real peers, because everyone you deal with is an employee, a customer, or a supplier. Moreover, the gap in skills and experience is often very large between the owner or CEO and the next level of management. You will probably not find your friends at work. Of course, you can develop other social networks outside work through professional organizations, clubs, religious and charitable organizations, and so on, but that takes effort and you'll likely be fully absorbed in running your business. This potential social isolation can be particularly troubling for owners who are unmarried. When we asked one CEO of a small business whether he was married, he emphatically told us he was *very single*!

Resources and infrastructure

Finally, large organizations have all kinds of resources to support their employees' work: HR, legal, and R&D departments and plenty of capital to invest in new initiatives. The professionalism, procedures, and resources of larger organizations often mean that employees produce quality work. Smaller firms don't have the infrastructure and resources to support the standards found in large enterprises; therefore, getting it done generally becomes more important than getting it done *right*. As a result, for example, new products are introduced without the benefit of market research studies (the owner uses his or her best sense of the market); salaries are adjusted without compensation surveys (the owner calls a few friends who are owners of local businesses); financials are prepared internally and are not audited (the owner's information comes more from a daily involvement with every aspect of the company than from financial reports). As mentioned earlier in this chapter, many important decisions are made in small companies using intuition and limited data instead of careful and detailed analysis. While small-firm owners don't necessarily seek out these situations or approaches to doing business, these approaches are often necessities. But for these owners to be successful and happy, they must be comfortable with such intuitive, less data-driven decisions.

Skills and Traits

We've discussed some of the values and goals that need to resonate with you if you want to succeed as an entrepreneur through acquisitions. Now let's talk about the traits and skills we've seen in successful entrepreneurs.

Basic management skills

Many of the examples we highlight in this book involve MBAs from the Harvard Business School because they were our students and we know them well. But you don't need to have an MBA to follow this path. You do, however, need some management experience or at least some business acumen. You need to have an understanding of finance basics—financial statements and principles, and the basics of modeling.

You also need to know how to lead and manage others. You need to be able to make decisions, lots of them, even though you won't have all the information you'd like. Practicality and common sense go a long way in successfully managing a small firm. Finally, you need energy and focus, not just because leading a small firm is a lot of work but also because small firms are led from the front. The owner sets the pace and pattern, often taking on key roles such as director of sales and chief financial officer.

These basic management skills need not come from managing a business. We have seen, for example, great searchers and small-firm managers come from other career paths such as the military or engineering. Of course, not everybody has the skills to manage every business, and you'll need to find a company that you believe *you* can successfully manage after a proper transition period with the seller coaching you along the way.

A convincing attitude and confidence

Great communication skills are critical to an acquisition entrepreneur. You need to feel comfortable reaching out to people you don't know—sellers, business brokers, investors, your employees—and when you do reach out, you need to project an air of confident optimism. All of these people are deciding whether to believe in you. If they don't sense that you believe in yourself, why should they? Of course, this doesn't mean that you always feel optimistic or confident. But you know how to handle your worries. You need to make decisions and take action. Smaller-firm CEOs aren't frozen by a fear of making mistakes; they know they will make some bad decisions but will adapt and fix them.

Persistence

Especially as you are searching for the right business to buy, you need to have relentless energy: the willingness to keep looking for the right business, to keep researching each company you're interested in, and to keep negotiating again and again until you make your acquisition. When you are seeking out a business to buy, you might face months when you work 12 hours a day and simply not find a desirable prospect. It's a frustrating experience with lots of effort and no reward. Worse, you might find a prospect that you are excited about, reach agreement on price and terms, and work for months on closing the deal, only to have the transaction fall apart at the end because the owner decided not to sell. When you're searching, there are many frustrating days of little or no progress, some real disappointments and setbacks, and only one success that occurs at the very end of the process. Successful searchers keep working tenaciously through all the dramatic highs and lows of the pursuit and steadily advance toward an eventual acquisition.

Next Steps

A few lucky people absolutely know they want to run their own smaller firm early in their professional careers. For you, however, the decision may be complicated because whatever direction your career takes—owner of a smaller firm, manager in a large company, founder of a start-up—you'll be likely to find only a partial fit. Maybe you want to be your own boss but value your circle of professional colleagues. Perhaps you like the idea of a hardwired connection between effort and personal reward, but don't like being face-to-face with the risks the owner manages every day in a smaller business. Whatever your decision is, don't hold it to a standard that is unreasonably high. Most people who become entrepreneurs through acquisition sorted through similar conflicts.

As you contemplate your choice, consider this: While there are opportunities for personal wealth in this path, don't confuse prospects for your financial success with your satisfaction in the journey. Success is always hard to predict, particularly in a relatively unstructured career like entrepreneurial business ownership. Instead of banking on the numbers, focus on what your everyday life will be like in the different roles you are considering. Your vision of the journey is more knowable—and ensuring that you enjoy the journey will mean that the reward becomes icing on the cake.

Consider too that entrepreneurship through acquisition is, of course, the road less taken. Out of approximately 180 million Americans who work, fewer than 2% own their own businesses. But almost all of the successful entrepreneurs we know are happy with their jobs, while we know that many successful executives in big companies are not happy with theirs. And in our experience, we've never seen an entrepreneur who wants to return to working for somebody else in a large organization.

If you meet these qualifications—if this sounds like you—keep reading to learn more about the process of acquiring a small firm.

CHAPTER 3

The Acquisition Process

The process of finding and buying a company is likely to be one of the most interesting and challenging experiences of your professional life. Interesting because you will learn about many different businesses, meet all types of people, and think through decisions that will shape the direction of your career. And challenging, both physically and emotionally, because until you buy a business, there is no end to the amount of self-structured work you can be doing. The process generally takes between six months and two years of full-time effort.

The rest of this book describes that process in detail, but this chapter will give you an overview so that you can understand what to expect—what the steps are, and how much time you'll need to invest and when. There are four phases, which we'll cover in the remaining sections of this book:

1. Preparing for your search

2. Finding the right business to buy

3. Making an offer

4. Completing the acquisition

Preparing for Your Search

Before you can even begin searching for a business to buy, you need to understand and plan for the cost of that search—both financially and in terms of other resources like time, energy, and lost income. Chapter 4, "Anticipating the Cost of Your Search," and chapter 5, "Paying for Your Search," will cover these financial costs in more depth and start you on the path to raising the funds you will need for both the search and the acquisition itself.

You will also need to identify the characteristics of the company you want to acquire. Some of these will depend on your personal needs, skills, and preferences—such as location, potential industry, and size. But we also have concrete recommendations about the kind of company that allows you to best manage risk: *an enduringly profitable small business that is established and growing slowly with recurring, loyal customers.* (See, however, the sidebar "What If You Want to Buy a Different Type of Business?")

Finding the Right Business to Buy

Once you have raised the funds for your search and gotten a sense of the kind of company you are targeting, it's time to begin. As you look for a company to buy, you will identify and compare literally hundreds of prospects at different times. Most of these you will review in a very

WHAT IF YOU WANT TO BUY
A DIFFERENT TYPE OF BUSINESS?

What if you don't want to buy just any small business but instead already have a specific business in mind? If you're a recent graduate from dental school, for example, you might want to buy an established practice. If you're passionate about antiques, you may have bought this book to fuse your avocation and a career by purchasing an antiques dealer—especially if your primary focus isn't financial success. Or if you're retiring from a role as an executive, you might want to settle down to run a small business in the community where you've lived for years.

Much of the process we describe in this book will work for you, too. Even though you've got a specific type of company in mind, you'll still need to find the right business. So, the searching and screening suggestions still apply, although the specifics might be different if your primary object isn't financial. For example, you might find prospects differently by placing your primary emphasis on trade shows instead of business brokers. You might also evaluate prospects differently, especially if your main measure of success isn't financial. Still, you'll also need to learn about the prospect, decide how much to offer, negotiate a deal, raise the money for the purchase, and then complete the acquisition. We'll take you through each of these steps in this book.

preliminary way before dismissing them, efficiently eliminating those that don't meet your criteria. A few more serious candidates will get more attention, and by the time money changes hands, you'll want to know everything about the target company—its financial performance, suppliers, workers, managers, customers, equipment, industry, competitors, and so on.

Identifying prospects

Finding small businesses that are available for purchase—a task we call *sourcing*—is the first step. As you begin your search, you will need to decide whether you will primarily identify these opportunities through business brokers or by reaching out to owners directly. Each approach involves a different process.

Owners who have decided to sell their companies will often retain business brokers to help because most of these owners are first-time sellers. The brokers typically manage all aspects of the process, including negotiating terms and price, for their clients. The broker also puts together documentation about the company; the information can help you as a buyer identify early on if the purchase isn't for you. Once a broker gets to know you, they may also reach out to you if a company comes their way that matches your interests. Most searchers keep in close contact with 100 or more brokers during their search; the broader your search—the more industries and geographical locations you consider—the more brokers you need to work with.

Some searchers find their own deals by contacting small-business owners directly, without a broker involved and without knowing in advance whether the owners want to sell their businesses. This approach circumvents the broker process and may result in better deals at better prices because the companies aren't on the open market. Contacting owners directly is an especially time-intensive approach, however: You'll need to assemble your own lists of business owners, conduct research on the web and elsewhere, and then try to contact them, whether by mail, email, or cold call. You'll need to contact numerous small-business owners to find a willing seller—far more than if you are going through a broker. And once you do find a potential business to buy, you will often need to educate the seller about market terms and conditions. Without a broker, there's only you to educate the owner, and the process becomes time intensive. We'll discuss managing brokered and direct searches in chapter 8, "Sourcing Prospects Using Brokers," and chapter 9, "Sourcing Directly."

Filtering prospects

However you source your options, you'll need to quickly eliminate most prospects to narrow down your larger list into a smaller, more manageable set of businesses that you want to learn more about. To filter your prospects, you'll use information that is readily available from the broker or the owner and evaluate prospects against the characteristics of the businesses you want to buy. In chapter 10, "Enduringly Profitable Small Businesses," and chapter 11, "Using Financial Information to Gauge Enduring Profitability," we'll explain this process and give you the tools you need to judge the soundness of a business so that you can decide whether to pursue it more seriously.

Making an Offer

Once you find a small business that seems intriguing, there is a lot to learn to evaluate if it really is a good company for you to buy. How does the business really work? Who are its customers? Are there any key employees or suppliers? You'll dig deeper into the documentation given to you by the broker—or, if you have sourced the prospect directly, you'll get more information from the owner. You will begin to speak with the owner, visit the company, reach out to other firms in the industry, and more. As you do your research, you will either learn that you should eliminate the company from consideration or decide that you want to keep learning more. This *preliminary due diligence* is iterative, as every answer to a question often raises more questions as you dig into the business. You'll keep up this pattern—learn, filter, ask more questions, learn, filter, ask more questions, and so on—until you are ready to make an offer. This is the heart of the search process, which we'll cover in chapter 12, "Filtering for the Owner's Commitment to Sell."

Offer price and deal terms

While there is no magic formula to get the right price for your company, most small businesses sell for between three and five times their adjusted earnings before interest, taxes, depreciation, and amortization (EBITDA). That's a concept we'll explain more fully in chapter 11, but think of it as similar to the company's pretax operating cash flow. This formula will vary, of course, according to the company's value to you (and to its value to the seller). Considering these factors, you'll send the seller a first offer for the company in an *indication of interest,* or IOI. The IOI is usually just a one-page letter that contains few details about the proposed transaction other than price and isn't binding on either the buyer or the seller. The purpose of an IOI is just to get an agreement on pricing, even if it is just a range, before investing time on the other terms and conditions of the offer. We discuss pricing and the IOI in chapter 14, "How Much Should You Pay for a Small Business?"

The letter of intent

In addition to pricing, you'll need to decide on other terms of your proposed acquisition, like the amount of seller financing. The buyer and seller often negotiate the specific price and other terms of an acquisition. That process begins with a formal letter (called *a letter of intent,* or LOI) that contains the important terms of your initial offer. These negotiations often center first around price and then move to other financial arrangements, contingencies, a plan for confirmatory due diligence, and an agreement with the owner granting you exclusivity for a few months as you make your preparations to buy the company. You'll learn more about deal terms and getting to a signed LOI in chapter 15, "Deal Terms," and chapter 16, "The Offer."

At the same time that you are negotiating the LOI, however, you'll need to continue to source other potential deals through brokers and direct outreach and conduct preliminary due diligence on these other companies. You must keep your pipeline full and other deals moving forward because most LOIs are not accepted by the seller. Sometimes the sellers have unreasonable price expectations or aren't really committed to selling; other times, they need more cash and reject seller financing or turn down the deal for other reasons. Often, you never know their reasoning because you get the famous "Wall Street no," which is just silence—that is, the owner never responds to your offer.

Completing the Acquisition

Once you get a signed LOI back from the owner, you will continue to conduct further research into the organization to confirm that your understanding of its finances and operations are correct—a phase we call *confirmatory due diligence*. This phase is the most time-intensive portion of the search and acquisition. You'll be spending even more time at the company than before, to learn everything you can about it. You'll finally gain access to employees, suppliers, and, hopefully, customers.

At the same time, you will be meeting with lenders and equity investors to raise funds for the deal (see the sidebar "How Will You Pay for Your Acquisition?"). You will also hire and manage outside professionals for various important tasks. For example, you'll need an attorney to prepare the formal acquisition documents and to watch out for hidden liabilities. You'll want an accountant to review the financials and to prepare a quality-of-earnings report so that you can be sure that the company has been paying its bills and taxes and is likely to be profitable in the future. There might be other outside professionals you'll need to consult (and pay) to learn about, for example, environmental liabilities or labor issues.

Often, issues that buyers uncover during confirmatory due diligence change their view of the company. As issues arise, you'll need to track them down quickly. If there is a deal breaker, you want to find it quickly to manage your time and to save on outside professional expenses. For example, accounting results may need to be adjusted due to a mistake by the owner, and you will need to seek a price modification. These renegotiations are not always

HOW WILL YOU PAY FOR YOUR ACQUISITION?

You don't need to use all your own money to fund your search or to buy your own business—and you don't need to have rich friends, either. Some of the purchase price will come from a bank loan, some will come as a loan from the seller, and the rest will be equity that you will raise from individual investors.

Who are these investors? More people are qualified to invest in the equity of your business than you might think: Individuals in your community—doctors, lawyers, owners of other small successful firms, and executives—may be good candidates for investors. These people have accumulated wealth but rarely have access to private company investments that offer much more attractive returns than do public stocks and bonds. We repeatedly see first-time entrepreneurs through acquisition raise equity by networking among individual investors like these, and in chapter 5, we show you how to approach such investors for your acquisition, your search costs, or both. Part V describes how to raise these different components of the money you'll need to complete your acquisition.

successful; when a deal fails, you'll need to move on to other potential acquisitions in your pipeline.

If your confirmatory due diligence work is successful, however, you will negotiate a purchase agreement that defines the acquisition in even more precise and detailed terms than the LOI. We'll cover these steps in chapters 16 through 19.

One day, you'll finally close. Entrepreneurs by acquisition describe this step as momentous and hugely rewarding: Their months of patiently sourcing, filtering, and negotiating have finally culminated with the acquisition of a business—their business. They are now a CEO and an owner. But their work isn't over: It has just begun. Their next few months are often described as "like drinking from a fire hose" as they assume responsibility for their company while continuing to learn many new details. We'll give some final advice for this transition phase in chapter 21, "The Closing Days and Beyond."

Next Steps

The search for a small business is all about creating opportunities through outreach and then bringing energy and enthusiasm to those opportunities to find the right deal for you. You will need to be totally committed to the search: There can be a lot of disappointment along the way, and until you actually close on an acquisition, you have little to show for your efforts. That is why the traits we highlighted in chapter 2, "Is Entrepreneurship Through Acquisition for You?," are so important. It will take energy, enthusiasm, tenacity, and the ability to motivate yourself every day to be successful in your exploration and to finally close on the company that is right for you.

PART TWO

Preparing for Your Search

You are intrigued with the concept of becoming an entrepreneur by buying a small business that you will own and run. This part of the book takes you through the preparation for the search. We begin with **chapter 4, "Anticipating the Cost of Your Search,"** and describe both the out-of-pocket costs and the opportunity costs of lost income as you search full time. We then focus on how to get the money to successfully complete your search in **chapter 5, "Paying for Your Search."** Finally, in **chapter 6, "Identifying the Characteristics You Want in Your Business,"** we describe the characteristics of the business that you should buy.

CHAPTER 4

Anticipating the Cost of Your Search

The first step in buying a small business is to find companies that are for sale at a reasonable price and that match the characteristics you want. We call this task *searching,* and much of this book explains how to search effectively.

You'll discover that searching can be both time-consuming and expensive and that success depends a lot on your judgment and a bit of luck. Searching is difficult because the market for small businesses is opaque and fragmented. Potential sellers are reluctant to announce that their business is for sale, lest customers and employees begin to consider other options. So, you'll either need to work through fragmented and secretive business brokers or reach out to business owners directly in hopes that they might be interested in selling. Plus, the set of businesses available for purchase keeps changing as some businesses are acquired and other owners decide to sell. As a result, this exploration phase can take as much as one to two years of full-time effort.

As you seek out companies for sale, you will incur costs such as office expenses, communication and internet charges, travel and data expenses, and professional fees for lawyers, accountants, and other experts. But the biggest cost of the search is the need to put your existing career on hold and forgo the compensation you would otherwise receive. This compensation includes your salary, any bonuses you might receive, and your benefits such as health insurance and pension contributions.

The price tag on your search depends how you decide to organize it. As we will describe, the resulting range of costs is very wide, from over $1.0 million to less than $500,000. Some of the costs are out of pocket, like the fees paid to accountants and lawyers, but most of the costs are your forgone salary and benefits. You can get investors to pay some of these expenses, or you can pay for them yourself, sometimes in novel ways, like relying on your spouse's job to fund living expenses. But before you decide whether to raise funds for your search, you need a better sense of the parameters of your search.

Deciding on the Parameters of Your Search

To determine the cost of your search, you need to make certain decisions about how you will organize it:

☐ Will you search with a partner or alone?

☐ Will you focus your search by geographical location or industry?

☐ Will you primarily use a broker, or will you do your own sourcing?

There is no one best or most efficient way to search for a small business to acquire. We have seen potential entrepreneurs succeed with broad national searches and other people do well with highly focused regional searches. Jay Davis and Jason Pananos, for example, spent over 2½ years and $750,000 searching for a company before successfully completing their acquisition of Vector Disease Control International. At the other end of the time spectrum, it took Jude Tuma only 2 months to find his acquisition, Penn Warranty, and another 3 months to finalize the acquisition. The most frugal entrepreneur that we are aware of is Ari Medoff, who spent less than $25,000 in both search and personal expenses during the 14 months he spent looking for a company on the Southeast coast of the US. Ari successfully acquired a home nursing care business that nicely matched his search criteria, but he and his family spent much of those 14 months living in his in-laws' basement apartment. Some of these differences are due to luck, but others are related to decisions the people made about the type and scope of their search.

Searching alone or with a partner

Many searchers, especially those who are more inexperienced, decide to search with a partner and are certain that a team approach is best. They argue that the partners provide essential feedback to each other—that two heads are better than one. They also reason that a partnered search will be more than twice as productive as a solo search. And much of these arguments is true:

If partners have complementary skills, the person with the most relevant experience can examine each deal: Manufacturing companies can be reviewed by the partner with the operations background; retail opportunities can be assessed by the partner with a marketing background. Ongoing conversations between the partners also sharpen their search skills as they share experiences and refine their focus. We believe the synergy between partners is real and potentially substantial.

But, of course, two heads require two hats. Though a search has some fixed costs such as data acquisition and setting up a website, the inclusion of a partner generally doubles the expense of searching. There are two salaries forgone, two people requiring living expenses and health insurance, a bigger office, twice as much travel, and so on.

Searching with a partner incurs another huge cost: The financial benefits of entrepreneurship are divided in half because two partners now share the upside. The company will also need to support two salaries and two benefits packages—significant ongoing expenses for a small business. It also can be difficult to divide responsibilities: What will the two of you do? Typically, you'll be buying the company from a single owner. Who will be CEO? What will the other partner do? How will disagreements be resolved?

One way to circumvent some of the challenges of a partnered search is to look for a larger company to acquire—one big enough to have sufficient financial rewards and complex managerial challenges for two partners. But we believe bigger small companies tend to trade at higher prices relative to their profitability and cash flows, so even with this approach, the economics of being a successful entrepreneur through acquisition are far more challenging in a partnered search.

However, most people who search as partners don't choose a partnership for economic reasons. Instead, we think they expect that their partner will help smooth the emotional ups and downs of a difficult process. Searching can be lonely and full of daily disappointments; of course it helps to have somebody with whom to share these troubles. But as you make your decision, be careful that you aren't using a cost-benefit analysis to rationalize taking on a partner just because you want the emotional support. A partnership is very expensive; your search will cost twice as much, and your benefits will be cut in half.

In perhaps only this instance, we think Gordon Gekko in the movie *Wall Street* offered some sage advice: "If you need a friend, get a dog." A dog is much cheaper and will give you unconditional love even if you don't find and close a deal quickly.

The scope of your search

You might be tempted to consider every available deal when you are looking for a small business to buy. You might think that limiting yourself to a particular geographical area or industry at the outset would curtail your choices, perhaps leading you to miss an outstanding acquisition because you didn't even know about it. But a national search across dozens of industries is time-consuming and expensive. You would have to evaluate thousands of potential deals nationwide in a wide range of industries to identify those that are worth a closer look. And there is the time and expense of traveling to distant parts of the country to learn more about promising opportunities.

Sometimes, searchers limit their scope to a particular location because they have strong preferences about where they live. Entrepreneurs need to live near their businesses because they will work long hours and be deeply involved in every aspect of the business for a decade or more. Absentee owners, especially with newly purchased companies, are asking for trouble. If you and your family cannot happily live in the surrounding community, you will probably be miserable at home, less effective at managing your business, and less successful overall. If you are unwilling to live where a potential business opportunity is located, then there is no sense searching for businesses there.

An industry focus lets you take advantage of your background in a particular business. We often see acquisitions in a "business next door," that is, a business that is similar to one that you've worked in previously. You'll know where opportunities are likely to be present and where there are unmet customer needs. You might even know a willing seller of a business that interests you or have a network of industry contacts that can help guide you to a potential target. An industry focus will also take you less time and effort to understand the target business and to see in a potential target the value that others might not see at all.

How you'll source prospects

Your search begins with finding small businesses that are available for purchase—a task we call *sourcing*. Your approach to sourcing, like the decisions to have a partner or focus your search on a particular location or industry, will have a big impact on the costs of your search. There are two approaches people typically take to source potential deals; we will describe these approaches in detail later in chapter 8, "Sourcing Prospects Using Brokers," and chapter 9, "Sourcing Directly." In this section, we just sketch the approach and outline the associated costs.

The most common and straightforward approach to sourcing is through brokers. Owners—most of whom have never sold a company before—retain brokers to help sell their company. Brokers help sellers through each step of the sale. From the searchers' perspective, brokers help to identify committed sellers and make it easier to learn about the prospect. If the prospect seems to be a company you would like to buy, the broker can help get the deal completed, which is especially helpful when the owner is a first-time seller. If a prospect is offered by a broker, it indicates the seriousness of the owner's intention to sell— an important factor in the efficiency of the search.

Many searchers rely exclusively on brokers as they look for a company to buy. If you don't source through brokers, you'll need to contact business owners directly about potential sales. The upside of direct sourcing is potentially better deals on better firms—because these firms generally won't have been available to other searchers on the open market—but the downside is that direct sourcing is far more expensive. You'll need to try different outreach methods, from individual cold calls to mass-produced messages to personalized letters following significant research into individual companies and their owners. The vast majority of these outreach efforts go nowhere, largely because most owners are not interested in selling their businesses. The least personal of approaches gets about a 1% response rate; targeted, personalized efforts do better but, of course, take much more time.

Direct sourcing is a manufacturing effort of sorts. You will need to hire two or three people to work full time to help with the volume of outreach, and while these positions can be minimal-cost internship opportunities, the scale of the operation still requires a larger office with more telephones, computers, and other infrastructure. A direct approach also requires the purchase of company data to help identify potential targets and professional-grade databases to track the large volume of outreach and responses.

On its face, using brokers is much more economical than direct sourcing. Moreover, it is critical that you minimize the time and expense devoted to simply identifying prospects. However, some smart, successful people do source directly. Many of these pursue a hybrid approach that combines both brokered and direct sourcing. With such an approach, you first learn a lot about the big picture by looking at brokered deals: for example, identifying interesting market niches. Focusing on those niches can then make direct sourcing more productive since you'll be more familiar with the industry and, consequently, better at evaluating prospects. You can use your network within the industry to connect with potential sellers, and you'll come across as a more credible buyer.

Coordinating your choices

Some search structures make more sense than others. The two most common combinations that we have seen are (a) a directly sourced search with a partner, without a focus on a single industry or geographical location and (b) a broker-sourced search by one person who is focused on a particular part of the country. Other combinations, of course, can work, and we have seen that almost every combination can be successful.

Budgeting for Your Search

Once you have decided on the parameters of your search, you can begin to estimate your search budget. To keep it simple, we will look at the two common combinations just mentioned: a fully funded, partnered search that uses direct sourcing and a more frugal, self-funded individual conducting a regional search through a network and brokers. From these two extremes, you'll be able to base a budget for your own search on the parameters you have chosen. Table 4-1 totals the two-year costs for these two types of searches we are using as bookends. The costs for other combinations, of course, will fall somewhere in the middle.

We will walk through the budgets sequentially, that is, in the order that you will incur the expense. That way, you can follow the steps for actually getting started on your search and their associated costs. This will help you form both a budget and a to-do list.

Legal fees

You first need to form a company that you'll use as a search vehicle, because it broadcasts to brokers and potential sellers that you are serious about your search. It also helps keep search-related expenses organized and

TABLE 4-1

Costs of a two-year search to acquire a small business

	Type of search	
People	Partners	Individual
Scope	National	Regional
Sourcing	Direct	Broker
Out-of-pocket costs		
Legal	$25,000	$1,000
Office	$48,000	$12,000
Communication	$16,000	$6,000
Data	$20,000	$8,000
Travel	$120,000	$10,000
	$229,000	$37,000
Forgone income		
Forgone salary	$600,000	$300,000
Forgone benefits	$200,000	$100,000
	$800,000	$400,000
Reserve for broken deals	$50,000	$50,000
Total	$1,079,000	$487,000

keeps the legal and financial aspects of your search separate from your personal life.

In the United States, the company should be organized as a limited liability corporation (LLC). Outside the United States, most countries have an equivalent structure that you should use. These are pass-through entities—that is, the LLC itself does not pay taxes. Instead, the revenues and expenses make their way to your tax return and are taxed there. An LLC is simple to form: You can do it yourself using online resources or through an attorney at a minimal fee. Some law schools sponsor law clinics where aspiring lawyers will form your LLC for you at no cost as practice. You will also need an employer identification number (EIN) (or equivalent) from the Internal Revenue Service (IRS). You can obtain the form yourself and request the number from the IRS.

Before you can form your LLC or get an EIN, you will need to come up with a name for your company. We recommend that you keep it professional so that you can get on with the actual business at hand—finding a company to buy. Skip the stupid or cute names, no ex-lovers, current lovers, or dogs; you are naming a company, not a boat. Of course, some names seem better than others. One of the best examples we have seen is Succession Leadership Capital, which was formed by Randy Shayler, whose sourcing strategy emphasized companies whose owners were nearing retirement. A word of caution: It is easy to invest a lot of time in finding just the right name, but it actually doesn't matter much. Once you have a name, be sure that it isn't already registered as a company and that you can get a domain name for your website and email address.

If you are searching alone and are funding the search expenses by yourself, then the name, obtaining an EIN, and setting up the LLC is all you need to do on the legal front. We estimate about $1,000 in legal expenses, less if you do some of it yourself or find others to do it at reduced costs.

If you are planning a partnered search with a national scope, you will also need an operating agreement to govern the relationship between you and your partner. If you plan to get outside investors to fund your search efforts, you will also need a shareholders' agreement that specifies the rights and responsibilities of the limited partners who are your investors and the general partners who are the two searchers. These agreements can be simple or complex, depending on the nature of the relationship between the general partners and the number of limited partners. Typically, there is a simple agreement among the general partners but a more detailed agreement between the general partners and limited partners. Those agreements can easily consume $25,000 in legal fees.

Office expenses

Solo searchers usually begin by working out of their homes, especially if there are no small children at home. If that's not possible, you'll need to get a humble office in which to work. It can be as simple and low cost as you can endure because no outsiders will visit your office. You don't need a conference room, kitchen, lobby, reception area, and the like. Reliable telephone and internet along with basic utilities are the requirements. A window is a luxury. The office is just for you, and you'll be paying for it: Be frugal. Imagine a 12-by-12-foot space, an old file cabinet, an older metal desk with a telephone and computer on top, a worn-out chair, and a pull-chain light. Even if your regional search is centered on an expensive city location, your office doesn't have to be; if you are searching out of New York City, think the far reaches of Brooklyn, not Times Square. In Boston, think Allston, not Copley Square. We are pricing your individual office expense at $6,000 per year.

If you have a partnered search or plan to use interns in a direct search, then you need more space and it has to work for others in addition to yourself. The space will need to be better equipped and more convenient. You might want a small conference room, multiple offices, probably a few windows too. Our guess is that you'll need 600 square feet of office space and that it will cost four times the simple, dark 12-by-12 space a single searcher would use, say, $24,000 per year.

Communication

You will need a telephone system with conference calling, forwarding, and voicemail capabilities, and if you are doing a partnered search or plan on having coworkers help you with sourcing, you'll need extensions as well. Don't just rely on your home phone or everyone's mobile devices—you and your employees will be on the phone a lot throughout your search, and you need something that is reliable and static-free and has a decent speakerphone and comfortable headset.

You will also need a website that brokers, potential sellers, and investors can visit to get a sense of your professionalism. You can build a site yourself using a variety of different software aids, or you can hire somebody to do it for you. You should include information about yourself, your search approach, and your investors or advisors; visit websites of other searchers to get a feel for typical standards. As with choosing the company name, there are no rewards from investing heavily in a website—just keep it professional and simple. You'll also need to have an email address that matches your website; again, keep the email separate from your personal account to signal that you are engaged in a serious, full-time, professional search.

Finally, you'll need a database system that allows you to keep track of your phone calls, emails, and leads and the companies you have pursued. Simple web-based systems are available for just a few dollars per month through companies like Zoho.com; these are sufficient for a single searcher using brokers to source deals. A bigger search process—such as partnered search or direct sourcing—may require a more powerful system such as Salesforce.com, which will be more expensive, perhaps costing more than $100 a month.

Company data

There are many associations and networks of business brokers that allow you to easily contact their members to source deals for free. In addition, new online systems that connect searchers and brokers, such as Axialmarket.com or Dealnexus.com, streamline this process even further. Brokers can use the system to look for likely buyers and can send searchers potential deals according to the characteristics the searchers identify. These systems cost about $4,000–$5,000 per year for searchers.

If you will be reaching out to companies directly, you will need a substantial amount of information about thousands of small companies because you won't know, before you contact them, which owners might be interested in selling. While some searchers try to economize on data by guessing at owners' email addresses, this is not a good use of your very scarce time. A better approach is to buy data; in addition to saving time, this enables a more personalized search approach with higher response rates.

Travel

With a regional search, travel to a potential acquisition is likely to require just a few hours in your car and, perhaps, some inexpensive motel rooms. It isn't going to cost much, perhaps $5,000 per year.

In a national search, travel expenses are much larger. As you begin your national search, you will probably visit a potential acquisition once or twice a month. When you find one that interests you, it will usually take several trips to the company as the sale process progresses. These trips are likely to be multiday adventures with plane travel, taxis, dinners, hotels, and the like. While the cost will surely vary by destination and duration, you can easily spend $30,000 on travel annually for each searcher.

Forgone salary and benefits

Searching for a company to acquire will require a full-time commitment to be successful. We understand why searching part time seems appealing, however. It would be so much easier if searching for a business to buy could be a hobby—something you could do on nights and weekends or in your spare time. That way, you could have a steady income from your existing job while you began your search to see if a good opportunity appeared.

The problem is that this approach doesn't work. There's simply too much to do. Take the first part of the process—sourcing prospects. If you choose a brokered search, you'll be contacting (and keeping in touch with) upward of a hundred brokers and looking at the thousands of teasers they send your way. If you source directly, the number of companies you'll need to contact is significantly higher than that. Even working full time, you'll feel rushed and overwhelmed—and will find a viable candidate perhaps once a week. Devoting only nights and weekends to this task will mean it will be a long time before you have found even a handful of businesses to research more closely. We know someone who has been doing this part time for years, and the effort has never come to anything.

The problem is not just the volume of work, but when you need to do it. Let's say you do succeed in finding a business to look into more deeply. As your research progresses and you move closer to a purchase, you need to be available and responsive. The seller needs to be able to meet with you at a convenient time to answer your questions, and you need to keep the process moving forward so he or she doesn't become frustrated and decide not to sell. You can't have a conversation with a commercial bank to talk about a small business loan at 7 p.m. And you can't wait until Saturday to call back a potential investor.

Leaving a full-time job is a big step, but it ensures that you have all the opportunities you can to find the right business and close on the deal on favorable terms. Still, it means that the largest part of your search cost is the salary and benefits you forgo. You know what you make for salary, so this is easy to calculate. Health insurance plus other benefits like pension contributions also need to be included. If you could otherwise earn a salary of $150,000, and assuming a 30% benefit rate, the opportunity cost of the search is about $200,000 per searcher per year. A partnered search would add $400,000 to the costs per year.

Obviously, the sooner you buy a company, the lower these and other costs are. But of course, you don't know how quickly that will happen. We recommend you conservatively budget for a two-year search. You are likely to close sooner, but budgeting for two years will help you focus on buying a quality company rather than racing against the clock.

Broken-deal costs

Once you find the company you want to buy, you will start incurring costs directly related to the deal—such as fees to lawyers, accountants, and other outside professionals. These costs can total well over $100,000. When you complete the acquisition, they get rolled into the total amount you finance to buy the business. But when a deal falls apart late in the process, you are responsible for the fees incurred by these professionals.

Some estimates suggest that about half the deals for smaller firms fall apart for one reason or another. If you follow the recommendations we make later in the book for staging your use of outside professionals, you can minimize broken-deal costs, but it is unlikely that you'll avoid all of them. To that end, we recommend budgeting a reserve of $50,000.

An insufficient reserve for broken-deal costs will lead you to become overly conservative so that you only retain professionals when you are completely sure the deal will be completed. At best, requiring that kind of certainty before you hire an attorney and accountant will lengthen the search process; at worst, you'll avoid potentially great deals because you have some resolvable doubts. Perhaps the biggest cost of not having a reserve for broken deals is that you'll be tempted to complete an acquisition even though you've learned some disturbing information about the company late in the process. You need to have the flexibility to abandon a bad deal throughout the process; no acquisition is far better than a bad one.

Next Steps

Whether you are considering the high end or the low end of these numbers, the totals suggest that the cost of searching for a small business is significant. You are probably wondering how searchers pay for their search. That's the subject of the next chapter.

CHAPTER 5

Paying for Your Search

Depending on the search parameters you chose in the last chapter, the cost of your two-year search may be over $1.0 million. Even if you search alone, use brokers, and keep your search focused, the two-year cost of your search is likely to be almost $500,000. Assuming that you are like most professionals, you probably don't have those resources at hand. This chapter focuses on how to get the money you need for your search.

A partnered, national search that uses direct sourcing usually requires raising money from investors at the outset of the search. The vehicle you'll use to raise that money is commonly called a *search fund.* It pays for the out-of-pocket expenses we identified in chapter 4 ("Anticipating the Cost of Your Search")—about $230,000 for the average partnered search—along with broken-deal costs plus a modest salary and benefits for the searchers. The salary it provides you is usually roughly $80,000 per year—less than what most searchers would make if they took a job—so that you also absorb some of the risk of not finding a company to buy and have a sense of urgency in your search. Usually, the fund is large enough to support up to two years of searching. So, the outside cash raised in a search fund for a single searcher who is searching directly and nationwide is about $300,000. The searcher effectively contributes the difference between $300,000 and the total costs of the search through a lower-than-market salary during the search. On average, partnered searchers raise twice that, about $600,000.

Some single searchers who have a regional focus and who rely on brokers decide to forgo raising money from investors to fund their search; these entrepreneurs seek capital from investors only once they have a deal in hand. We call that a *self-funded search.* The advantage of postponing outside investments is that more potential investors are willing to invest in a promising acquisition than in a promising searcher. That means that you can strike a better deal with investors by postponing fund-raising. But self-funding changes the nature of the search and can also reduce the likelihood of success.

Self-Funded Search

If you decide to fund the search yourself, frugality will need to govern your every decision. Self-funded searchers are usually willing to invest every penny of liquid assets they can muster to fund the out-of-pocket costs of their search; they will use any cash they have and borrow from their homes, their credit cards, and their retirement plans to get cash to fund their search. They do whatever they can to minimize expenses. Often, the searchers rely on their families to help fund their living expenses by depending on a working spouse or by living with parents because the searchers cannot pay themselves a salary or cannot use their limited cash for living expenses. Self-funding enhances the potential reward but surely also adds enormous stress to the already psychologically challenging search process.

As described in chapter 4, Ari Medoff self-funded his search and carefully minimized every expense, even going as far as living in his in-laws' basement for the duration of his search. He concentrated his search along the East coast of the United States from Pennsylvania through Georgia, which reduced his travel expenses (in addition to reflecting where he wanted to live). He used unpaid interns to assemble a database of smaller-firm owners and to conduct an emailing campaign. Instead of hiring a law firm to incorporate his acquisition entity Arosa, LLC, he used a law clinic operated by local university law students, who performed the service at no charge. His total out-of-pocket search costs were less than $25,000 for about 14 months of searching.

But it was a risky strategy with little flexibility. For example, when his acquisition fell apart just a few weeks before closing, the broken-deal costs nearly put an end to Ari's search. After a hiatus of a few months, he resurrected his broken deal and successfully acquired a home nursing care business in North Carolina. But his entire experience could just have easily not turned out so well.

Later in this chapter, we give some advice on approaching potential investors. But first, let's explore the choice of raising capital to fund the search.

The Search Fund

Search-fund financing provides greater resources for a more comprehensive national search. More importantly, if you don't have the money to search for one or two years, this path opens the way. You'll raise these funds by approaching investors who might be willing to contribute to the fund in exchange for a first look at investing in the target company as it is being acquired and a cut of the profits once the acquisition is complete. Investors contribute money and get a share of the profits; you contribute talent, effort, and time and get the other share. It's like agreeing on how to slice up a pie, except no one knows how big or tasty the pie will ultimately be when the agreement is made. Or if there will even be a pie: If the search doesn't result in an acquisition, investors simply lose their money.

The search-fund approach to becoming an entrepreneur through acquisition accomplishes three goals: First, it provides the needed funding for your search. The fund raises enough capital to pay for your out-of-pocket search expenses and a modest salary for two years. Second, it establishes a network of investors interested in providing equity capital for an eventual acquisition once you find the right business to buy. Third, sellers often ask prospective buyers to demonstrate that they can afford to buy the business; a search-fund group of high-net-worth investors is strong evidence that you can finance an acquisition.

David Rosner and Greg Geronemus created a search fund called Footbridge Partners in the fall of 2011. Greg had about a half decade of experience in the financial services and health-care sectors, while David had a similar length of experience working with a variety of smaller and midsize firms. Both men were committed to becoming entrepreneurs through acquisition, but both had spouses who were tied to the New York City area, so they planned a geographically focused search. They wanted to fund their search using investors. They began with individuals they knew and worked their way to a commitment of $550,000 in search capital from six investors. We'll follow their story as we show you how the process works.

Creating an offering memorandum

To launch the fund-raising process, you'll need to provide potential investors with a formal *offering memorandum* so they can understand your plan, the budget for your search, and the proposed terms for investors. When David and Greg created their offering memorandum, they had a lawyer look it over to make sure it was in compliance with the various regulations that govern investment fund-raising. Also, once they raised capital, their lawyer would need to draft a partnership agreement that followed the terms of the deal in their offering memorandum. For all these reasons, it's a good idea to have an attorney review the document.

Raising the fund

Once you have the offering memorandum in hand, your next step to raising a search fund is to find investors who might be interested in such an investment. Recognize that a search fund is an unusual investment, particularly when compared with the public market investments that dominate the portfolios of most high-net-worth individuals. That means you may need to expand your network to find enough investors interested in funding your search. David and Greg created a list of forty-five contacts who knew them and who either had the resources to invest or could connect them to people who might invest. The two partners started by reaching out to people on their list who knew them best. "Getting our first investor was the key," Greg said. "That person ends up serving as a reference for other investors because they know us well. Also, no one likes to be the first investor, but once you have an investor, it creates momentum."

Between October and December 2011, the two partners worked their way through their prospect list, sending emails first and then following up with calls and meetings wherever there was interest. "Each investor was different," David observed. "Sometimes, we would get a quick yes in our first conversation. Other times, we would have a whole series of meetings ending with a no. We probably could have been a little more decisive in putting aside prospects who didn't express strong interest early on." By the end, Greg and David had commitments for $550,000 of search capital from six investors. This was a smaller group of investors than is typical—a more common number is 10 to 15 investors, each contributing $30,000 to $50,000, but more importantly, the two partners assembled the capital they needed to fund up to a two-year search for a business.

Negotiating the terms

Most search funds have similar agreements between the searchers and their investors, but there is some variation. Here are the terms David and Greg negotiated:

1. If an acquisition was identified, the searchers were obligated to offer it to their investors.

2. If an acquisition was completed, the investors' original search investment (the $550,000) would be "rolled in" to the acquired company, and shares would be issued for that capital. Even if an investor chose not to invest in the acquisition, they would receive shares for their earlier round of capital. Most commonly, the initial search capital is rolled in at a 50% premium to reflect the risk of being in the initial round, so the entrepreneurs would have to repay $825,000 rather than $550,000 before participating in the profit pool.

3. The first proceeds would go to investors until capital had been returned, plus a payment of a minimum annual rate of return (usually in the range of 6–9% annually) called a "preferred return".

4. The two partners would share up to 35% of the remaining profit pool if the venture hit various return targets. In the Footbridge partnership,

there was also a catch-up payment to the entrepreneurs once the preferred return had been paid
to investors. This meant Greg and David would
collect up to 35% of the amount paid as preferred
return and 35% of all the remaining profits.

Closing the fund

The final step in the fund-raising process is to close the
fund. That's when documents that define the fund are
signed and when investors actually send the searchers
the committed funds. David and Greg closed their fund
in February 2012, about six months after they had begun
their fund-raising. With the money in hand, they began
their search. While they limited their search to the area
surrounding New York City, they used every available
means, including brokers, direct outreach, and local networking, to find prospects. In 2013, they identified and
acquired a 20-year-old travel company located in New
York City. The firm provided high-quality, exciting group
tour packages to some of the most fascinating countries
in the world.

Approaching Investors

If you decide to do an investor-funded search as Greg
and David did, you need to approach investors early in
the process to get the fund in place before you begin
searching. But even for self-funded searchers like Ari,
approaching potential investors early on will lay the
groundwork for reaching out to investors for acquisition
funding once you have a deal in hand. And even investor-funded searchers need to keep in contact with other

investors who might be willing to fund the acquisition itself. The search investors may be unwilling or unable to provide all of the funding you want at the time of the acquisition.

Let's now turn to specific recommendations that will help you move from an introductory meeting with a prospective investor to a commitment by them to invest.

Starting with people you know

Begin with family, longtime friends, clients, business associates, former or current bosses, and others who know you well. These people already believe in your personal capabilities, so you'll only need to sell the merits of your investment opportunity. With strangers, you'll need to sell yourself as well as the opportunity.

Starting with a group that is predisposed to believe in you has two benefits. First, you gain experience at pitching to investors in front of a supportive audience. Attracting investors is like most other tasks—you will get more skillful with more repetitions. Second, fund-raising works best when you take advantage of the network effect. No prospective investor wants to be the first one to commit; they derive confidence from the fact that others who know you well and have seen this opportunity have already signed up. That's how it worked for Greg and David. "Our first call," Greg recalled, "was on my former boss, who was very supportive. He decided to invest."

Then, when an investor commits, you should keep the momentum moving forward. For example, "I'm trying to build an investor group that works well together. Is there anyone you know who you'd suggest I speak to?" You will find that investors are very willing to share opportunities they like with their friends and colleagues. Again, Greg's former boss introduced the two searchers to other potential investors, some of whom invested in their fund.

If your personal network doesn't include a sufficient number of potential investors, however, you'll need to reach out beyond it. There is a community of investors who regularly invest in search funds and who generally welcome the opportunity to evaluate potential searchers and introduce them within their informal investor network.

Selling your search

Raising money is a type of sales call, and the fundamental rules of selling apply:

Arrive on time

This simple act communicates respect for the investor with whom you are meeting and quietly demonstrates that you are an organized person. One longtime investor in private companies commented: "If someone isn't able to arrive in my office on time, why should I believe they are capable of more difficult tasks?" Of course, no one invests in you because you arrive on time, but arriving late makes a terrible impression.

You should also send your offering memorandum to the investor at least several days before your meeting.

Look the prospect in the eye

You are selling your capability and confidence as the leader of a smaller firm, not just presenting an investment opportunity. Know your material cold—no notes—and turn the meeting into an eyeball-to-eyeball conversation between you and your prospective investor.

Tune into their language

Businesspeople speak a variety of dialects; you need to assess which one they speak and talk that way. If your investor is an expert in an industry that you are targeting, use the terminology of that business. If the investor isn't familiar with the business, brandishing buzzwords will signal to them that they are getting involved in something they don't fully understand, rather than proving how expert you are. Instead, speak in plain English.

Time your presentation

Early in the meeting, ask your prospect how much time they have. You should be flexible enough to adjust the arc of your story line to whatever time you are given. And you may have to keep readjusting: If the prospective investor asks questions, you may have to shorten your presentation again, whereas if they seem engaged and unhurried, you can add detail to make your pitch more compelling. Before the meeting, think through how to add and delete sections of presentation in response to your prospect's availability and level of interest.

Act like a peer

You want to establish a respectful relationship of equals. Investors want to back a CEO whom they respect, and they in turn want to be respected for the importance of their financial contribution and business experience.

Tell stories

One of the challenges when approaching investors is that many of the claims sound alike:

"I'm going to buy low and sell high."

"I'm looking for a business that has high barriers to competition."

"I'm going to improve marketing to generate more revenue."

Prospective investors who are infrequently pitched for private investments find abstract language like this unconvincing, while investors who do receive lots of pitches find this abstraction doesn't really differentiate one entrepreneur from the next. For either audience, staying general is not very effective. Instead, tell stories about different businesses that you have encountered.

Sharing relevant stories will accomplish three valuable goals: First, it breathes life into your plans by taking an abstract idea like "barriers to competition" and linking it to an understandable real-life situation. Compare these two ways of making the same point:

"I'm looking for a business that has high profit margins because it has high barriers to competition. This could be the result of high transportation cost, a well-known brand, or a reputation for not messing up."

Versus:

"I'm looking for a business with high profit margins because it has great barriers to competition. One business I looked at, Castronics, threads metal pipe for oil and gas drillers. The pipe is really bulky and heavy, so moving it around costs about six times what the actual threading costs, and as a result, competitors from outside the region are way more expensive. Also, it's really important to the drillers that the pipe arrives on time and that the pipe lengths fit together perfectly. For this reason, customers are really cautious about experimenting with other suppliers. That's why the company generates such attractive margins, and it's exactly the type of business I'm looking for."

In addition to engaging your listeners, sharing stories also gives them more information, making it more likely that they will follow your thinking and agree with your choice when you eventually come to them with a potential deal. One prospective entrepreneur we know illustrated for investors each of the characteristics she was seeking in an acquisition by briefly describing a business that she had screened and that had the characteristics. Later, when she described her proposed acquisition, investors often jumped in to say, "I see why you like that business—it has all the criteria you are looking for!"

Finally, weaving relevant business anecdotes into your presentation signals your own breadth of experience. A common question asked of every first-time entrepreneur is whether they have enough experience to become CEO of a business *now*. At some point in your discussions with investors, you will have to address this question directly, but before you do, it's valuable to create confidence that the answer is yes.

Indeed, in these initial conversations, it's not just the acquisition that's being evaluated; you are too. You are the prospective CEO of the company. These meetings are both investment presentations and job interviews, and investors will be assessing whether you are serious, hard-working, thoughtful, and mature. Be conscious of this, and convey these qualities in your conduct.

The Next Communication: Creating the Virtuous Circle

The end of each meeting is a key moment in which to manage momentum: You don't want your potential investors to feel rushed, but you do want them to believe that this investment has a time limit; they need to make a decision soon, or the opportunity will be taken by others. If prospective investors sense that there is no cost in waiting, they will simply defer making a commitment.

End each investor meeting with a proposal: "I'd like to give you a call in a couple of weeks to see if you have any questions and to update you on my progress"—and then follow up. When you do follow up, ask your prospect if they have any questions and then answer each question carefully before talking about how your fund is progressing. Momentum is a critically important ingredient when you are raising equity. Properly managed, momentum leads to a virtuous circle in which an investor commits to your plan, encouraging other investors to commit promptly so that they don't lose their opportunity.

Next Steps

You'll know from your budget work in chapter 4 how much money you'll need to raise. This chapter should have helped you decide how you'll fund the search, either by funding it yourself or relying on investors. Either way, you'll need to develop a network of investors that will either invest in the eventual acquisition if you self-fund or pay for the search and the acquisition if you raise a search fund. As you approach investors, you'll need to explain what kind of business you want to buy and why it is a good idea. That's the topic of our next chapter.

CHAPTER 6

Identifying the Characteristics You Want in Your Business

As you begin your search for a smaller company to buy, you might be tempted to think big thoughts about the future of humankind to identify the shifting sands of the business environment. You'll wonder, What is the next big thing? Where are the opportunities for big growth and fabulous profits? These kinds of musings make for wonderful conversations but rarely lead to good business decisions. In fact, we'll explain in this chapter that you should look for what may seem to be a *dull* business: one that has the same customers from year to year and is growing slowly—a business that is what we call *enduringly profitable*.

In this chapter, we will describe the kind of business we think you ought to buy and the characteristics you should consider.

An Established and Profitable Firm

As mentioned above, you should buy a business that has enduring profitability, that is, an established, profitable business model. A business is profitable when its customers are willing to pay more for its products or services than what the company must spend to provide them. It is that simple. What isn't so simple is why some businesses are profitable, year after year, while others struggle. Some struggling businesses were once profitable but are no longer. Others approach profitability but never achieve it, and some never enjoy even a glimmer of success. It is tempting to imagine buying a troubled business or one with uneven performance, because the purchase price would be very low. But we strongly advise against it, because you'll have to reinvent the business model and doing so is a very difficult and risky endeavor. Instead, buy a profitable business with an established model for success—one that is profitable year after year.

The essential characteristic of enduringly profitable businesses is recurring customers. There are, of course, many factors that make smaller businesses enduringly profitable. These include some important, basic management best practices such as treating employees and customers well, being honest, and keeping expenses low. Managing well every day is essential to building a good business. But a business that has enduring profitability is more than that. It is able to attract and keep the right customers, those who highly value its product or service and will purchase year after year.

When the ownership of a business changes hands, some customers may consider other choices, and competitors will quickly pounce on the opportunity. Buying a business and then losing customers is a nightmare. Our experience, however, is that recurring customers persist even when the ownership of the business changes. Customer retention is critical for a successful transition from the existing owner to a new owner. Those recurring customers provide the foundation for a great small business.

Slow Growth

Although high growth would seem like a wonderful characteristic of a business, it comes with high risk. High growth means that your new customers will quickly outnumber your existing ones. Because new customers bring new demands, there are many ways to get in trouble. New customers are, well, new; they have no loyalty to the company and no history. High growth requires great management effort. It also absorbs money rapidly, and raising that money puts a strain on the business and its owner. A rapidly growing firm also attracts competitors, which see the expanding market and the opportunity to attract new customers. So, in a high-growth business, you could work hard and still fail if you cannot keep pace with your competitors. And even if your business survives, you might find that competition has forced you to sell at low prices, so you enjoy little financial reward after all. Making this all the harder, the seller will demand a much higher price for a business that has the potential to grow quickly. Buy a high-growth business, and you'll work harder, face a bigger risk of failure, and pay more for the opportunity.

Low growth, in contrast, means low risk. And low risk is great because it is your money at stake. If you are like most small-business owners, all of your wealth will be tied to the company. Want to avoid worrying about paying college tuition for your kids? Buy a dull business. Want to work less than a dozen hours a day, seven days a week, every week, every year? Buy a dull business. You will still work hard and worry. But you should be able to have dinner with your family and sleep most nights. Why? Low growth doesn't put strain on management and doesn't require a lot of additional money. Things just move slower in an established business that is growing slowly. And in a slow-growing business, you'll have time to build lasting relationships with your customers. You'll learn what they value, and you'll adapt to provide products and services that they will appreciate. They will buy from you every year, and you'll learn to cherish that recurring revenue. It reduces your marketing and sales costs, but more importantly, it makes the sales next year less risky and far more predictable. That means fewer surprises and a much easier management challenge. Also, slow-growth businesses sell at lower prices.

As described in chapter 1, "The Opportunity: Entrepreneurship Through Acquisition," both Greg Ambrosia and Tony Bautista purchased seemingly dull businesses that grew slowly. Greg's business, a commercial window-washing service in Dallas, grows slowly because new high-rise buildings are added to the Dallas skyline slowly. His existing customers appreciate his good service and often use his company year after year, generating a stream of steady, recurring revenue. Tony's business, testing fire hoses, is similar; there is little organic growth in the market, but his customers almost always purchase his company's services year after year. Of course, both Greg and Tony can grow by expanding their service area and by attracting the customers from competitors by providing higher-quality services. But attracting new customers is often very difficult in businesses with repeat customers because the same economic forces that keep your customers buying from you keep your competitors' customers buying from them. Because gaining market share by winning over the competition's customers is so tough, your growth is likely to be slow but steady.

Buying a dull business doesn't mean your career as a CEO or owner is at all dull. Greg and Tony are fully engaged in a whirlwind of activities that make use of all their talents. Both men find that just running the business is hard work, with a myriad of challenges such as hiring employees, revamping the company's information technology systems, scheduling crews, improving the quality of their offerings, and professionalizing the business. And while growth is slow and steady, both Greg and Tony have expanded their capacity and are focusing on enlarging their company's customer base. Both often visit with customers to learn more about how to improve their offerings, and the two frequently meet with employees to improve safety, quality, and efficiency. Greg and Tony describe themselves as completely engaged, very busy, and constantly challenged because they know that they are ultimately responsible for their company's success.

Appropriate Size

We think it makes sense to buy a business with between $750,000 and $2.0 million in annual pretax profits. A few considerations should guide you. Because smaller businesses are usually less expensive to buy relative to their profits, they are more attractive. But you also want a business that is big enough to financially reward you for your efforts, and those rewards often depend on the profitability of the business, making larger prospects more attractive. At the upper end of our size range—$2.0 million or more in profitability—we find that institutional investors, like smaller private-equity firms, start to become interested and that competition raises the purchase price, reducing the financial benefits of owning the business. And finally, there is the practical consideration of how much equity funding you can raise. Generally, about one-third of your purchase will be funded by equity, and smaller firms often sell at roughly four times their pretax profits. So, at the low end of the range, you'll need to raise $1.0 million in equity, and at the upper end, almost $2.7 million. We'll explain how to do that later in this book, but if your personal network is small, it probably makes sense to focus on the lower end of the range.

A Good Match with Your Skills

Our suggestions so far—look for an established, profitable business with low growth, recurring revenue, and steady cash flow—leave hundreds of thousands of businesses for you to consider. But not all of those will make sense for you. We recommend that you take stock of your own background, skills, strengths, and weaknesses. Limit yourself to businesses that you will have the ability to manage.

Most businesses require general management skills—you'll need to understand a bit of everything: people, marketing, production, legal, accounting, and so on. Our experience is that most people with strong general management potential can thrive in a wide range of businesses. Still, if you are allergic to fur, don't buy a pet shop. Many businesses will require its owner to be its chief salesperson. If you hate selling or are not very good at it, don't buy a business that requires you to fill that role. Some businesses have facilities, customers, or suppliers widely dispersed around the world. If you are unwilling to travel, look elsewhere. If you don't like to manage people, don't buy a business with hundreds of employees.

You should know how a business works before you buy it. Investigate how the company makes its products or conducts its services and what these offerings depend on. Is there a key person? Does the seller possess some rare skill that you will have a hard time replacing? Is there an essential supplier relationship? You should also understand the customers. Why do they buy from the company? And you should know the industry. Are there competitors? What are the company's strengths and weakness relative to the competitors? You don't need to know all of this in the first encounter with the company; you will learn a great deal about a business throughout your search and when you give a particular company a closer look before buying it. But you do need to learn about it and understand why it is profitable before you close the deal. And there are, of course, some businesses that you will find easier to understand than others. But if you dig deep into the due-diligence process and the company's profile still seems like smoke and mirrors— and you can't get a clear vision of its strengths and weaknesses—don't buy it.

A Good Match with Your Lifestyle

There are also lifestyle considerations in your search. Make sure that you and your family are willing to move to the location of the business and can be part of the community. It is impossible to manage a small business successfully without being at the business almost every working day. At the same time, as you decide on the geographical scope of your search, don't put too-strict limits on where you want to live and work. We don't think it is sensible to look for a business in a narrow region— for example, a particular city or state is too restrictive. So, if your family refuses to live in North Dakota, don't look for a business in North Dakota. But if your family refuses to live anywhere outside of the western suburbs of Boston, perhaps instead of looking for a business, you should find a job nearby.

We emphasize your family's tastes for a reason: Running a business is all-absorbing. You have to put all of your efforts into making it a success. Your future and your family's financial security depend on it. You will not have the time to manage both the business and an unhappy family.

You also need to have the energy and focus to manage the business you buy. If you or your family has health restrictions or lifestyle preferences that will keep you from working long hours, you should be realistic about these limitations when searching. One of the great things about owning your own company is that you get to make your own trade-offs about how hard you work and how much money you make. You can choose to make less and spend more time with your family without having to ask anybody's permission or apologize to anyone. Business owners are in the unique position of being able to structure their professional life in a way that suits them and their families. We know of people who decided to become business owners because they could run their businesses successfully while still having the flexibility to pursue other commitments or passions. This flexibility is one of the most wonderful things about being a business owner. Think about those preferences as you are searching to make sure the business you choose allows you to pursue them.

Buying a Business, Not a Job

There are all kinds of ways to become your own boss, and the life you lead is clearly dependent on the path you choose. Some people accomplish professional independence by owning a business; others through self-employment—they are independent salespeople, business brokers, literary agents, electricians, interior decorators, freelance consultants, or any of hundreds of other professions. But the earnings of any job are eventually limited by the number of hours in a day. There are only so many customers that an individual can serve. You can add assistants who might extend your reach, but as long as the customers value most the contributions of a particular person (you), it is a job, not a business. In a successful business, customers value the products and services from the *company*. The company develops systems and policies so that individual providers can be substituted when one person moves on to another position. The customer recognizes the importance of the company, and that is what makes a business more than a job.

There are surely some jobs that are much better than some businesses. We know of two interesting examples—a computer services company and a website design firm. Both companies had a common operating philosophy of not having a central office and keeping overhead extraordinarily low. The CEOs were the nexus of their businesses and assigned tasks to employees and subcontractors directly. These executives were also the primary salespeople and financial managers of their companies. There was no level of middle management. The streamlined chain of command helped make both of these businesses very profitable, and both CEOs earned more money than they had before they became CEOs. But did they have great businesses—or great jobs? Different people might see the answer to that question differently, and it could be the subject of a lively debate. But, sadly, in these cases, we know the answer. The CEO of the computer service company was in a serious auto accident, and the CEO of the website design company had a personal health crisis. Both were unexpectedly and completely away from their companies for months. When they returned, their businesses were a shell of what they had been: Most employees had left, clients had not paid, and almost no new work had been sold. Without the CEOs, there were no businesses. These executives had had jobs—great jobs, but still just jobs.

There is, of course, nothing wrong with buying a great job. But this book focuses on buying great businesses that are more than jobs because we think owning a great business is much better than having a great job. We have two reasons for thinking this is so.

First, when you are the owner of a smaller firm, your earnings are unhitched from the hours you work. This makes you different from craftspeople or other professionals who essentially bill by the day or the hour; ownership gives you the potential to earn much, much more. Your reward is tied to the management structure that you create and that enables others—hopefully, many others—to deliver the products and services that your customers value. Such a structure potentially gives you not only larger monetary rewards but also a more flexible lifestyle.

Second, when you own a business, you get paid in two ways. You are paid for being the manager—think of this as the annual salary you would make if you performed this same job at someone else's company—and you also earn a return on the money, time, and energy you have invested in the company. If you are successful, the sale of your business will be an important part of your wealth. When most professionals retire, their income stream rapidly comes to an end. They have no ongoing business to sell; they work to make money, and when the work stops, so does the money. Successful craftspeople sell their tools upon retirement for less than they paid for them; a successful company will sell for much more than the amount that was put into it.

So when searching, look for a business, not a job. Avoid companies in which the owner has an essential role in the delivery of the business. It is common for owners to be the company's primary salesperson, but be wary when the owner is involved in the delivery of every product or service the company provides. If you cannot imagine a smooth transition from the seller to yourself because the seller seems so irreplaceable, you might be looking at a job, not a business. Avoid businesses in which your work would be so irreplaceable that the company would be worth nothing when you decide to leave.

What to Ignore

Our shopping list of the desirable features of a suitable business acquisition excludes some items that you might have expected. We did not suggest, for example, that you restrict your prospects to businesses that you are passionate about. Wooden boats. Old cars. Windmills. Music. Rare books. Fine foods. Wine. The list is long and different for each of us. Some searchers believe that the business they run should have a social purpose, for example, reducing carbon emissions. We appreciate all of these desires to mix a professional career with a larger passion, but passion for a business is an elusive concept at best and, at worst, will cause you to overlook problems with a business and overpay. You should be passionate about making money and building the professional life that you desire. Hobbies and social causes rarely make good businesses. It doesn't make sense to require that you love the products or services of the company you buy. Remember: Dull is good. We also excluded price from the shopping list. The price of the business you buy isn't restricted to the amount of cash you have in the bank.

Next Steps

As we will explain later, there are many ways to finance an acquisition, including traditional sources such as borrowing money from a bank and less traditional sources such as funding from outside investors who will share the risks and rewards of the business with you. So, there is no meaningful price limit on the company you buy—though, obviously, the higher the purchase price, the less of the company you will own personally. And while you can buy a company that far exceeds your personal wealth, the company has to be a good value. The next few chapters are devoted to helping you recognize a good value in a potential acquisition.

PART THREE

Finding the Right Small Business to Buy

You are now ready to begin your search in earnest. This part of the book takes you through the first two steps of the process: sourcing prospects and then filtering them to quickly eliminate the unattractive ones so that you have time to thoroughly study the few that might make good acquisition candidates.

We begin with **chapter 7, "Managing Your Search Effectively: An Overview,"** which focuses on how to apply filters to the prospects you source. We'll describe how searchers find potential companies to buy using brokers in **chapter 8, "Sourcing Prospects Using Brokers,"** and directly contacting owners in **chapter 9, "Sourcing Directly."**

Then the next two chapters help you further filter your prospects down to those with enduring profitability and committed sellers: In **chapter 10, "Enduringly Profitable Small Businesses,"** we explain the underlying traits of good small businesses with enduring profitability; in **chapter 11, "Using Financial Information to Gauge Enduring Profitability,"** we turn to the numbers and show you how to use financial information to do so quantitatively. Judging whether a seller is committed or not—the other key trait of attractive prospects—is covered in **chapter 12, "Filtering for the Owner's Commitment to Sell."**

CHAPTER 7

Managing Your Search Effectively: An Overview

As you begin your search, you'll need to juggle two closely related tasks. First, there is sourcing—finding small companies that are acquisition prospects. While you are looking for just one good acquisition target, you'll need to source at least hundreds—yes, hundreds—of prospects that are available before you find one that is right for you. Second, there is filtering: You'll need to learn enough about these prospects to eliminate the companies that will not be good acquisitions for you. To search efficiently, you must be ruthless and quickly reject weaker prospects so that you can spend time learning enough about interesting acquisition opportunities to make an offer.

Sourcing

Whether you choose to source through brokers or go directly to owners, you will need to build a system that generates a steady stream of prospects throughout the time you are searching. It will take a month or two for you to build momentum, and after that, sourcing will be a largely repetitive task through which you'll discover, on average, two new prospects every day.

As your search progresses, keep refining your sourcing efforts to more efficiently find the deals that are the most interesting to you. You might, for example, discover that certain brokers specialize in particular industries or geographical locations that intrigue you, or you might focus on a specific industry that you believe has particularly attractive prospects.

As you search, don't get so excited about a particularly attractive prospect that you devote all your time to it and stop sourcing new prospects. Most exciting prospects eventually become far less exciting: Perhaps you discover that the historical results are much weaker than originally represented, or perhaps the prospect has lost several large customers, or perhaps you and the seller cannot negotiate agreeable terms of the sale. Whatever the reason, sometimes it takes months to eliminate a prospect. If you stop sourcing, you'll have to restart sourcing. The restart will take a month or two, needlessly delaying the successful conclusion of your search. It is much better to maintain your sourcing momentum and add new prospects every day up to the day that you finally close on the small company you acquire.

Filtering Prospects

Efficiently filtering the new prospects you source is one of the most important tasks in the search process. Most of the business you source will have to be rejected quickly for you to have sufficient time and resources to learn more about those that seem to hold greater promise. Filtering is an iterative process. There are *initial filters* that you can apply quickly and with very little information; for example, you can eliminate a prospect for its unattractive location or industry almost immediately. When the prospect survives the initial filters, you'll then apply *deeper filters* that require a bit more information about the business and bit more time to form a judgment about the business or its seller. Eventually, either the prospect will be eliminated on the basis of readily available information in the filtering process or you will decide the prospect is worthy of more scrutiny. This next step—preliminary due diligence—is covered in part IV of this book, "Making an Offer."

Initial filters

Your initial filters should be based on simple information about the prospect—information such as a basic description of the business, its size, and its location. For prospects sourced through brokers, this information will be readily available in *teasers,* one-page summaries of businesses up for sale. Teasers offer the first information you'll learn about the prospect, and this information is often sufficient to eliminate the business from consideration. For directly sourced prospects, some of the information for the initial filters will be available from business directories and other public listings—indeed, you may glean enough information from these sources to eliminate a prospect before even attempting to contact the owner. For the businesses you do contact, you'll apply the initial filters using the information you receive during your first call with the owner. Whether you are applying your initial filters through a teaser or the information you glean from the first call with a directly sourced prospect, it is usually a very quick process. For companies that you can eliminate because of a feature like location, the filtering might take less than a minute. Other filters will take more time, but in general, you should conclude within an hour or two whether a prospect satisfies your initial filters.

Your initial filters are reasons to quickly eliminate prospects. In the last chapter, we described some features of the business we think you should search for. Use the initial filters to apply those characteristics to quickly reject the prospects that don't measure up. Some aspects of firms, like enduring profitability, will not be readily apparent and so won't be first on your list to investigate. But others, like the overall profitability of the prospect, are easy to determine. Your initial filters should answer these simple questions:

- ☐ Is the prospect consistently profitable?

- ☐ Is it an established business instead of a start-up or turnaround?

- ☐ Is it in the right size range?

☐ Is it located in a place you are willing to live?

☐ Do you have the skills to manage it?

☐ Does it fit your lifestyle?

If you can answer yes to these initial questions and the prospect also survives any additional filters you choose to apply, it is time to apply deeper filters.

Deeper filters

Here are the two most important questions that you want to answer when applying your deeper filters:

☐ Is the prospect enduringly profitable?

☐ Is the owner serious about selling the business?

While it's too early in the process to expect definitive answers to either of these questions, you are trying to make a quick preliminary assessment, which will require a closer reading of the materials or a conversation with the broker or owner and some judgment on your part. Brokers can provide more information about the prospect either in a phone call, an email, or a *confidential information memorandum* (a more detailed written description of the prospect). For prospects directly sourced, information is more difficult to obtain. You can request financial statements from the seller and then talk with him or her to learn more about the business. With any of these methods—information from brokers, financial statements, direct communication with owners—you are not trying to learn everything you can about the prospect; instead, you want to learn just enough to eliminate it.

The first deep filter to apply to a prospect is an assessment of its enduring profitability. An essential characteristic of a smaller company with enduring profitability is that it has customers that regularly buy from it again and again. But because you do not yet have access to historical customer lists at this stage of filtering, you need to infer what you can about recurring customers from the information that you do have. Try to figure out why customers buy from this company instead of its competition and why they don't use the presence of competition to drive down the company's profit margins. In chapter 10, "Enduringly Profitable Small Businesses," we will identify specific business characteristics associated with recurring customers and, in turn, with smaller companies that have enduring profitability. Chapter 11, "Using Financial Information to Gauge Enduring Profitability," provides some quantitative filters you can apply to also get a sense of a company's enduring profitability.

The second deeper filter we recommend is that you evaluate the owner's willingness to sell. As we mentioned earlier, for most owners, this will be their first experience selling a business. As they make this journey, they will learn a lot. They will learn how much their business is worth. They will learn the risks and requirements of normal deal terms. They will reflect on what their lives will be like after the business is sold. For all these reasons and more, it is not uncommon for a business owner to change his or her mind about selling, even after considerable effort has been expended by both buyer and seller.

The sellers aren't being deceitful; they are learning as they go. But if you've spent several months working with a seller and learning about the business, you have paid a heavy price for their education if the deal doesn't go through. So, we recommend making an early judgment about an owner's commitment to sell and only pursuing the prospects whose owners are serious about selling. In chapter 12, "Filtering for the Owner's Commitment to Sell," we offer some guidance on how to make this assessment.

Next Steps

The initial and deeper filters help you eliminate prospects that will not be good acquisitions for you. If you use these filters efficiently, most of your time will be devoted to learning more about the companies that survived these filters. As you study these companies, you're likely to come up with more questions about each business than you have answers. Keep track of those queries—if a prospect still seems interesting after you've spent a day doing research and applying the initial and deeper filters, those questions will form the basis of the next step in the process, preliminary due diligence. We'll cover that in chapter 13, "Preliminary Due Diligence," but first we'll describe the sourcing and filtering processes in more detail.

CHAPTER 8

Sourcing Prospects Using Brokers

In December 2009, Patrick Dickinson and Michael Weiner closed on their $9.6 million purchase of Castronics, Inc., an oilfield services provider based in Kimball, Nebraska. Neither of them had ever been to Kimball; Patrick had grown up in Pittsburgh, and Michael in a Cleveland suburb. Both came from families that were not involved in business or entrepreneurship. Patrick's father was a doctor, his mother a homemaker. Michael's father operated a law and accounting practice, and his mother was a speech therapist. The two young men became friends in their first class as undergraduates at Duke University but went their separate ways professionally after graduation. Michael worked for a large bank and later returned to Cleveland, joining a firm that invested in small and midsize businesses. Meanwhile, Patrick worked for an investment group that was acquiring and operating waste management companies across the United States.

In 2008, Patrick and Michael's ongoing discussions led them to partner in searching for a small firm to buy. With each partner quitting his job and living off personal savings, they began an energetic search across the country to acquire a small firm as quickly as possible, and in about six months, they acquired Castronics. They attribute their quick success to their exclusive reliance on sourcing prospects through brokers and thus owners who, in Patrick's words, "were really serious about selling their companies."

We agree. Sourcing through brokers is the most successful approach to overcome the problems presented by uncommitted first-time sellers. Brokers also provide organized information about the companies for sale, making it easier for searchers to quickly apply initial and deeper filters to prospects.

Good brokers are much more than just a listing service of businesses for sale. A great business broker will provide critical information about the seller's commitment to sell and background about the company. Moreover, brokers help manage the seller, organize the sales process, and help resolve disagreements between the buyer and seller. Brokers also are helpful coaches to first-time sellers, guiding them through each step of the sale. When the buyer asks for more details about the historical financial results of a company, a good broker is there to explain to the seller that the buyer is not accusing the seller of being dishonest and that testing results and assumptions is simply part of the buyer's quest to learn more about the business. By acting as an intermediary, a broker will dampen the emotional ups and downs that come with selling a business and will help make the sales process more orderly. A good broker might make the difference between a successful acquisition and one that collapses.

Finding Business Brokers

There are approximately 3,000 to 4,000 business brokers in the United States. Some sell very small enterprises like pizzerias and gas stations while others focus on businesses valued at up to $20.0 million. Some brokers specialize in a particular industry, although most will represent almost any business. All brokers work on a commission that is paid by the seller. Sometimes there is a monthly retainer, but most of the fee is paid when a transaction closes.

Brokers are not hard to find; in fact, they want to be found. Most are members of the International Business Brokers Association (www.ibba.org), the Association for Corporate Growth (www.acg.org), the Alliance of Merger & Acquisition Advisors (www.amaaonline.com) or the Association of Professional Merger & Acquisition Advisors (www.apmaa.com) and these membership lists are easily accessible. Brokers that specialize in a particular industry usually advertise on that industry association's website or in its publications. Most brokers can also be identified by searching the web for "business broker," "merger and acquisition advisors," or "buying and selling businesses." Many searchers find the online system Axial (www.axialmarket.com) useful, because brokers can use it to find likely buyers and can send them potential deals based on the characteristics the searchers identify.

Introducing Yourself to a Business Broker

You should expect to call hundreds of brokers as Patrick and Michael did during their search. When you introduce yourself to a business broker, these are the most important things to communicate:

- ☐ You have access to the capital to acquire a business.

- ☐ You are determined to buy a company and expect to complete an acquisition soon.

- ☐ You are a professional and a credible business buyer.

- ☐ You are looking for a specific type of company to buy (describe the size, industry, and type of business such as manufacturer, distributor, or services provider).

Marketing yourself to brokers is an important part of your communication with them. As Patrick recalled, "They get a lot of calls from tire kickers, so we have a short pitch we make about how we have the determination, expertise, and capital to close on a company."

Rod Robertson is the managing partner of Briggs Capital, a mergers and acquisitions advisor that brokers small- to medium-size privately held businesses. He confirms the importance of presenting yourself well to a broker. Rod receives about 100 contacts a year from individuals interested in acquiring a business. When he talks to prospective buyers, he is evaluating them on behalf of his clients: "I'm eventually going to present a handful of potential buyers to my client, who is the business owner. I want that client to feel like I've done a good job selecting folks who are highly professional, present themselves well, and could credibly buy and run the seller's business."

"Tell me about your financing," Rod likes to ask buyers who contact him. "That scares off about a third of them." As a prospective purchaser moves further along in the process, Rod probes their funding further: "If you've got investors interested in backing your acquisition, I want to speak to a couple of them to make sure *they're* serious. I don't want someone getting to the finish line and scrambling to raise their equity."

Evaluating Businesses Presented by Brokers

If your initial outreach is successful, the broker will send you information about businesses, usually by sending a teaser. As described earlier in the book, a teaser is a one-page summary that usually describes the business and gives an overview of the prospect's financial performance.

The teaser

Teasers provide enough information to apply your initial filters—basic information about the business, its general location, and its financial performance. That information will allow you to filter out about 80% of the teasers you receive. At this stage, you are looking for reasons to say no. You'll probably review a lot of teasers, spending on average 10 to 15 minutes on each document. Patrick and Michael, for example, reviewed about 750 teasers.

Because brokers place low priority on keeping track of searchers interested in buying a business, they won't remember you unless you work at it. Once brokers start sending you teasers, stay in touch. Call them periodically to see if they have any new companies for sale and to remind them of your areas of interest. Also, take the time to explain why you have rejected particular companies they offered you—it will help educate them about the type of business you are looking for and communicates that you are reviewing their offerings seriously.

As you review teasers, evaluate not only the companies they describe but also the quality of the materials themselves. Since anyone can become a business broker, there is a wide range in their capabilities. While you should look at all of the teasers you receive, you should give more attention to material from brokers you've already identified as better. Often, it becomes clear that some brokers are a better fit for you simply because they are more productive in highlighting businesses you find attractive. Perhaps they focus either on industries or regions in which you are most interested, or maybe you have established a good rapport with them and they are especially helpful as you follow up with questions. Increase your frequency of communication with these brokers. But at the same time, keep your broker network broad; any individual broker only markets a handful of companies each year, and it is impossible to predict which broker will be the source of the prospect you eventually acquire.

The sidebar "Example of a Teaser Offered by a Business Broker" contains one of the hundreds of teasers that Randy Shayler reviewed in 2012 during his search for a business to buy. The teaser is representative of the kind that might pass your own initial filters. First, as the teaser shows, the company was consistently profitable, with profits dipping slightly between 2009 and 2010 but then growing substantially between 2010 and 2011. (The teaser's projections for 2012 and 2013 showed this profitability persisting and expanding slowly, but you should be skeptical about the reliability of those forecasts.) Second, the prospect was an established business roughly in the size range that Randy was interested in; a purchase at 4x 2011 EBITDA would be $4.0 million, an amount he believed he could finance with a combination of bank debt, seller debt, and investors' equity. He liked the idea of living in the Northeast, although he would need to know the company's precise location to be sure. He also thought he could manage the business and, in fact, was intrigued by rental businesses generally. As for lifestyle concerns, Randy liked the connection to education and anticipated working long hours at whichever business he purchased.

For prospects that pass the initial filters you applied to the information in the teaser, recontact the broker to request more information, which is typically contained in a *confidential information memorandum* (CIM). This document is much longer than a teaser and will give you more information about the company and its industry, facilities, products, customers, and financial results. Because the CIM contains confidential information, you'll

EXAMPLE OF A TEASER OFFERED
BY A BUSINESS BROKER

A Leading Regional Provider of Musical Instrument Rentals, Sales and Educational Services

This is a unique opportunity to acquire an established **musical instrument rentals and sales business** operating in the Eastern United States. This dealer primarily serves the education market in its region and has an ideally situated, multiuse facility with ample room for growth, including a warehouse, office space, retail store, repairs department, and private lesson rooms. The company has enjoyed consistently profitable financial performance for several years and projects over **$3.5 million of total revenue** and **over $1.6 million of adjusted EBITDA** for the year ending December 31, 2012.

The acquisition of this company offers an ideal platform opportunity for an acquirer with or without a strategic operating company. An investor or a financial acquirer would benefit from a stable, established business that still offers considerable opportunities for improvement and growth, while a well-positioned strategic acquirer could achieve territorial expansion; could add significant school programs, affiliates, and sales rep relationships; and could extend into desirable new product and service lines as well.

**EXAMPLE OF A TEASER OFFERED
BY A BUSINESS BROKER**

Products and services

- Inventory of 16,000-plus rental musical instruments

- 12,000-plus rental contracts currently in place

- Fully stocked rental and retail inventory in the following categories: string instruments (violin, viola, cello); woodwind instruments (clarinet, trumpet, saxophone), as well as a complete line of other new, used, and vintage musical instruments available for sale in the company's retail store

Financial Performance Summary

	2009	2010	2011	2012p*	2013p*
Total revenue ($ millions)	$3.4	$3.1	$3.3	$3.5	$3.7
Adjusted EBITDA ($ millions)**	$1.1	$1.0	$1.5	$1.6	$1.7

Note: Data shown above and throughout this confidential summary profile was obtained from unaudited financial statements, internally prepared financial statements and projections, and the company's management estimates, and is used with permission.
*2012p, 2013p: projected performance for 2012 and 2013, respectively.
**EBITDA: earnings before interest, taxes, depreciation, and amortization, adjusted to reflect pro forma add-back of certain onetime discretionary expenses.

probably need to execute a nondisclosure agreement before the broker will send it to you. When Randy had some questions for the broker about how the business worked, he signed the required confidentiality agreement and then received the CIM.

The confidential information memorandum (CIM)

The CIM is the broker's major work product. These memos are generally about 40 pages long. For example, the CIM Randy received for Zeswitz Music was 50 pages long (we don't reproduce it here because of its length and confidentiality). Going far beyond the teaser, a CIM offers a detailed description of the company's business activities, assets, employees, customers, competitors, historical financial results, and future projections. While a CIM provides a very useful overview of a business, it is also important to recognize that the document is a marketing tool prepared by brokers who generally do not confirm the accuracy of the financials or other company information presented. When filtering prospects, however, you can assume that all of the rosy assessments and descriptions in the CIM are accurate and, in light of this information, evaluate the company using your deeper filters (you will do more due diligence later). At this stage, you are looking for some indication that the business is enduringly profitable and that the owner is committed to selling. We'll explain how to apply those deeper filters in later chapters. Because the CIM emphasizes the most favorable characteristics of the business and the owner, if the business doesn't meet your deeper filters according to its CIM, you know it's time to move on.

Further conversations with the broker

If the prospect survives the deeper filters in light of the information in the CIM, contact the broker to get more information, particularly around areas where you have the most concern about the memo's accuracy or completeness. Here too, try to find reasons to say no. Michael Weiner described the process he and Patrick Dickinson used: "We would prepare five to ten questions from the CIM and interview by telephone the broker or, if possible, the seller themselves. We were aggressive about killing deals." Sometimes the broker will be able to answer your questions directly; sometimes they will go back and forth, acting as a conduit between you and the owner, and sometimes they will arrange a telephone interview for you with the seller.

The conversations between Randy and Zeswitz's financial advisor, Sharif Tanamli, confirmed many of Randy's initial impressions from the teaser and the CIM. He learned the name of the company, Zeswitz Music, and its exact location—Reading, Pennsylvania, about 60 miles from Philadelphia. Randy's wife was a college administrator, and the proximity to Philadelphia made Reading an attractive location because of the nearby schools. He also learned that the company was a well-established business—it had been in operation since 1923 and was the second-largest musical instrument rental company in Pennsylvania.

Overall, the information he collected convinced Randy that Zeswitz Music met all his initial filters. He also believed that he could use the information in the CIM, together with conversations with the broker and the owner, to apply the deeper filters about enduring profitability and the owner's commitment to sell.

Next Steps

Randy found Zeswitz through a broker. The other way to find potential acquisitions is by directly contacting company owners. We turn to that approach in the next chapter.

Ultimately, no matter how you find prospects for acquisition, you'll need to apply the two deeper filters: enduring profitability and owner willingness to sell. The remainder of part III will examine these two steps in detail.

CHAPTER 9

Sourcing Directly

In May 2012, Ari Medoff completed his acquisition of Nurse Care of North Carolina, a home health-care agency located in Durham, North Carolina. He found Nurse Care after eight months of sourcing prospects by directly contacting business owners. Ari explained why he chose to reach out to sellers directly as part of his sourcing strategy: "We did some outreach to brokers. But by directly approaching owners, I was able to see opportunities before they were widely shopped. I also avoided the competition of a broker-run auction." Also, he wanted to live in the Southeast, where he had been raised, and in a smaller city, where he could raise his family and become a member of the community: "I grew up in a tight-knit family of six children in Greensboro, North Carolina, where my dad was a doctor at Duke Hospital and my mother a stay-at-home mom." Direct sourcing would allow Ari to incorporate his strong geographic preference into his search.

Searchers who focus on direct sourcing often say they get better pricing and find better companies. They also form a stronger personal relationship with a seller. Good relationships are particularly important in the small-company marketplace because sellers usually have no experience selling companies and are often surprised by standard deal terms. A broker can help mediate a transaction, but in their absence, a friendly, trusting relationship with the seller supports the give-and-take that gets deals done.

There are two early, essential steps when you are sourcing prospects directly. These steps are not required when you source through brokers. First, direct sourcing requires that you find owners who are interested in selling their businesses, while with a brokered search, the fact that the owners have retained a broker is at least some evidence of their commitment. Second, direct sourcing requires you to collect, on your own, enough information about the prospects so that you can reject some of them. In a brokered search, on the other hand, that information is contained in the teaser and confidential information memorandum (CIM).

Finding Interested Sellers

Direct sourcing requires that you communicate with thousands—yes, thousands—of companies' owners to find those who are interested in selling their businesses. This task becomes a numbers game because it is very difficult to learn much about a small, private company and its owner without talking with them, but very few—usually 5% to 10%—are interested and willing to have that initial conversation. With the willing owners, however, your outreach will be warmly welcomed. These become your prospects. Of course, most of these contacts will not pass your initial and deeper filters, but remember, you are only looking to buy one company.

With a direct approach, you use business directories and online databases to identify the thousands of businesses you'll need to contact to identify just a few interested parties. Once you have selected the prospective businesses, use some combination of emails, direct mail, and phone calls to reach out to them. Email has a practical advantage over trying to cold-call business owners by telephone, even though the latter might at first seem like a more personal approach: Business owners tend to have receptionists or voicemail as gatekeepers on their telephone; your email, on the other hand, is likely to reach "owner eyeballs."

However you approach it, direct sourcing is an intense and time-consuming process. Searchers who direct-source usually use unpaid interns who are assigned tasks of assembling mailing lists and sending out emails or letters to business owners. These interns are typically recent college graduates who are looking for business experience to burnish their résumés. They spend from three months to one year working full time on an acquisition search—the searchers we have spoken to report that interns are not hard to find. Because interns require management and coaching, it is best to employ full-time and not part-time interns or, at a minimum, interns who can commit a meaningful number of hours each week.

Your message to owners

With a direct-sourcing approach, you need to balance reaching a large number of prospects with generic messages on the one hand and crafting personalized messages that generate a higher response rate on the other. Ari Medoff took a hybrid approach that allowed him to do both.

First, he and his interns created a large email list with 20,000 names of smaller firms located in the areas he wanted to live in. They assembled the list from a variety of sources, including internet listings, business directories, local chambers of commerce lists, and so on. He emailed thousands of owners of these firms, introducing himself and describing his objective very generally. Ari's typical email read like this:

[Seller's Name]:

You probably receive lots of letters, phone calls, and contacts from brokers, investment bankers, competitors, accountants and "deal makers." *This is different.*

I'm an entrepreneur backed by a number of prominent investors and private-equity groups who is looking to *purchase and run one company.* I would move to [Seller's City] and become the manager of [Seller's Company Name].

If you're thinking about exiting from your business and want to explore a quick, flexible transaction, please call or email me. My information is below.

Thank you,

Ari Medoff
Telephone: 919-555-0111
Website: www.example.com

Over the several months of this generic but far-reaching campaign, Ari saw a response rate as low as 0.5%—similar to the average response to direct mail.

At the same time that he was sending this generic message, Ari also created a set of much more personalized emails. Because each message required more time and effort, he didn't send out as many; however, the response rates were better. Here is an example of one of his more customized communications:

Walter,

Congratulations on Caldwell Products' 25th anniversary. I'm sure that 25 years ago you never could have imagined that today the company would service over 1,200 clients in 41 states. Great news on the State of Illinois deal.

As Caldwell Products is a leading player in software and services for the public sector, I'm sure you probably receive a lot of letters, phone calls, and contacts from brokers, investment bankers, competitors, accountants, and "deal makers" who are looking to turn a quick profit but who have no idea about you or the needs of your company.

This letter is different because I am an energetic entrepreneur with a long-term focus, looking to purchase and run one great company. I am backed by a number of operators and investors. If a transaction were to occur, I would move to the Minneapolis area with my family to lead the company.

I have work experience in business development with start-up and established tech companies. My MBA from the Harvard Business School and master of public policy degree from the Kennedy School and the backing of a number of prominent investors and equity groups are additional reasons we will build on the success you have had to date.

If you're thinking about exiting from your business and are interested in exploring a quick, flexible transaction, please call me at 919-555-0111 or email me at xxx@ example.com. You can also visit my website at www .example.com.

Thank you,

Ari Medoff

Like Ari, once you have assembled your list of prospects, you will need to determine the right combination of personal messages and mass mailings to reach out to owners. You could randomize how your messages are assigned, but you might more reasonably target the more personalized messages to prospects that seem more appealing, for example, in light of their location or industry.

Filtering Prospects

Once a business owner signals interest in selling, you need to learn enough about the prospect to decide if it is interesting to you. You'll follow the same filtering process as with a brokered search, but you need to find your own information to evaluate the prospect; without a broker, there is no broker-prepared teaser or CIM. Most searchers schedule a telephone call with the prospective seller as the first step in assembling the information that will be the basis of their filtering.

The first call

The easiest way to begin to gather the information you'll need to filter prospects is to speak with the owner. While there's an enormous amount that you need to learn about the business, the owner is unlikely to give you much information at this point, and you can only focus on so many things at once. Owners are especially sensitive about sharing any detailed information about financials. Therefore, with this first call to the owner, focus on three goals.

First, as with a brokered search, you need to establish your credibility as a buyer. You need to quickly make the owner feel that you are someone to whom they could imagine selling their business. You should leave the person with an impression of your management skills, humility, willingness to learn, and energy—and access to capital. For Ari, his geographic focus helped: "I found that owners all took me more seriously when they learned I was from the local area."

Second, you need to assess the owner's interest level in selling the company. The risk of an uncommitted seller is far more acute than it was with a brokered approach—you are now, after all, dealing with owners who may have never thought about selling, not ones who hired brokers to sell their businesses. Gently probe the owner's interest in selling. Although an assessment of the owner's commitment is one of your deeper filters for prospects sourced through brokers, there is a much higher likelihood of an uncommitted seller among directly sourced prospects. Consequently, getting information early about the owner's reasons for selling is especially helpful. Selling is a big decision for business owners, and real sellers are usually able to specifically describe their motivation. We'll provide guidance on elucidating and examining these reasons in chapter 12, "Filtering for the Owner's Commitment to Sell." Although you also want to learn early on if the owner has a realistic valuation for the business, this first conversation is too early to accomplish that. Before you can discuss value, you will need to obtain the company's financials and determine the annual cash flow it generates.

Third, you want to begin to gather information to apply your initial filters. For example, make sure that the business is in the size range that works for you. If it is too small—profits below $500,000—it probably isn't worth your time. If it is too big—profits above $3.0 million—you'll probably be unable to acquire it for a reasonable price and the acquisition will require more fund-raising and associated complexity than we recommend for a first-time buyer. Of course, prospects are not going to reveal their company's profits to a stranger, but you can get around this by asking some general, high-level questions about the business: How long has the company been in business? Why do customers select it? What are the competitors like? How many employees does the company have? From the owner's answers, you can extrapolate whether the company is likely to fall into your size range.

Armed with the information you gathered in the first call and the information about the prospect's location and industry that you gathered before the call, you should be able to apply your initial filters. As the call ends, if it seems that the prospect passes the initial filters, be sure to keep the momentum going. "This has been a good call. I really appreciate your time, and I'm excited about your business and its potential. Why don't we both give it some thought? May I call you next week? We'll probably both have some questions we've thought of in the meantime."

If the prospect does not pass your initial filters, try to use the conversation to generate additional leads. Small-business owners know other small-business owners and may well know other businesses that might be good prospects.

A warning: You will find prospects who seem interested in discussing a sale, and in the very first call, invite you to visit them as a next step. It's tempting to accept; it can feel like you've just gotten a sharp tug on your fishing line. But it's much too soon to visit unless the owner happens to be a short drive across town. You will exhaust your time and resources if you visit every owner who expresses interest in meeting you; just because the owner is interested in selling doesn't mean the company is an attractive acquisition. You need be confident that the prospect meets your initial and deeper filters before you get on a plane.

Next Steps

As you continue to work with a prospect, move toward signing a nondisclosure agreement; then the owner can send you some historical financials. This may take a while because owners will be reluctant to share confidential information. But having those financials in hand, together with your conversations with the owner, is like having a CIM; you'll be able to apply your deeper filters to see if the company is enduringly profitable or if there is a reason to say no. You can learn about the company's profitability, stability, growth, and thus its value to you. As you go, you'll generate more questions to ask the seller, such as the reasons behind any year-to-year changes in revenue, expenses, and profits. You'll use that information to assess whether the company is enduringly profitable—which we'll discuss in the following two chapters.

CHAPTER 10

Enduringly Profitable Small Businesses

Our first and most important recommendation about characteristics you want in your business was that you buy an enduringly profitable business with an established model for success—one that is profitable year after year. In this chapter, we offer some guidance to help you translate that concept into practical diagnostic tools for working through your deeper filters.

Since recurring customers are the foundation of an enduringly profitable small business, we suggest that your first deeper filter be whether its customers buy from your prospect again and again. Usually, you will get detailed qualitative information about the company either in the CIM for a broker-sourced prospect or through a longer conversation with the owner for a directly sourced prospect. This information could include details about the company's reputation, its business model, and its past history. Look for indications that the business has an outstanding reputation: That is the simplest reason why customers would keep returning. Other reasons should also be readily apparent from business descriptions: Some businesses integrate with their customers' internal systems in a way that makes it expensive for the customer to shift suppliers, for example. Other companies have an important role in the customers' businesses but constitute a small expense for customers, so that there is no reason for the customer to seek out a competitor with a lower price. All of these characteristics create a bit of pricing advantage for the business while also reducing risk that competitors could poach customers.

Reputation

A company's reputation for excellence keeps its customers from eyeing the competition. Take Be Our Guest (BOG), a party equipment rental company located in Boston. BOG rents tables, chairs, linens, plates, glasses, and cutlery to caterers. At first view, BOG could be taken for an undifferentiated commodity business. After all, you'd think caterers would simply rent from whoever had the lowest rental rate on their inventory of party equipment.

And yet, BOG has loyal customers that return year after year. Why? The answer is that failure is extremely expensive for BOG's caterer customers; far more expensive than the likely price difference between BOG and its lowest-priced competitor. Imagine that it is the wedding day for Mrs. Parkington's only daughter, and you're the caterer who has been hired to produce the dinner. You've used BOG before, but with 300 guests, you're considering switching to an unknown competitor with a lower price. But then you start to think. What if something goes wrong at the reception? What happens to your fee if the equipment you need doesn't show up on schedule? And what about the damage to your future business after Mrs. Parkington tells all her friends what a lousy caterer you are and how you ruined her daughter's wedding and perhaps her whole life? You know and trust BOG, and you realize that its reliability is worth every penny.

BOG is a business that is small for a good reason: The market it serves needs to stay relatively small. The party equipment rental business is regional because it requires intensive management to constantly solve little service problems (before they become big). This sort of management does not lend itself to a geographically distributed operation. If the business starts serving caterers too far from its warehouse, its ability to respond quickly deteriorates while its transport costs rise and eat into profit. BOG's scale may be limited, but it has a great reputation. So, despite its small size, it is an enduringly profitable business because of this solid reputation.

No Competitors

While BOG differentiates itself from its competitors with its reliable reputation, Castronics is a wonderful example of a company that has *no* meaningful competitors simply because of its location. As described in chapter 8, "Sourcing Prospects Using Brokers," Patrick Dickinson and Michael Weiner used brokers to source their prospects and ultimately acquired Castronics. The company specializes in providing threading, perforating, and refurbishment services for pipe that is used in the oil and natural gas industry. Located in Kimball, Nebraska, the company primarily serves customers in the Rocky Mountain and upper Midwest regions of the United States.

The pipes the company works with are typically 40 feet long; on average, one unthreaded tube costs roughly $1,000 to manufacture and $300 to transport, while threading it costs only $45. As a result, customers care much more about transportation costs than threading costs. What makes Castronics special is that it is located near active drilling regions where there is great demand for threaded pipe; Castronics is the only company providing this service in a 500-mile radius. Its location thus gives Castronics a substantial advantage over its more distant competitors. So customers continue to buy threading services from Castronics, year after year, and the company faces little price pressure from competitors. That is a recipe for a company that will be profitable for the foreseeable future.

What if another threading company enters the geographic market that Castronics serves? Such a move is not impossible, but a new competitor would have to overcome a few hurdles to be successful. First, it would need to obtain the licenses and certifications to cut the different threads required by Castronics customers. Second, it would need to find a location that offers efficient transportation and distribution, preferably near a railroad siding. Third, the competitor would need to attract the appropriate workforce, a task that Castronics devotes significant efforts to accomplish in its rural environment.

And perhaps most importantly, the competitor would have to convince potential customers that it can reliably provide the service in a timely manner, because delays and defects are costly and potentially dangerous at the drilling site. While none of this would be easy, a company could overcome these hurdles, and because of this potential for entry, Castronics cannot charge whatever it wants to for its services. Instead, Castronics has to be careful not to encourage competition. Still, because the barriers to entry in its market are so high, Castronics does have comfortable profit margins and recurring customers.

The Importance of Being Unimportant

Customers always want lower prices. But when it comes to demanding lower prices, customers will focus first and hardest on their biggest categories of spending. An automobile manufacturing company is going to focus far more resources on making sure it has the most competitive deal from its steel suppliers than on reworking a deal with the company that provides its postage meters. Thus *the importance of being unimportant:* If the small business you buy provides something that only makes up a small portion of its customers' expenses, then those customers are much less likely to switch to other suppliers.

Vector Disease Control International (VDCI) of Little Rock, Arkansas provides insect control programs to municipalities mostly in the southeastern United States. Municipal governments relentlessly try to reduce costs, putting out to public bid most goods and services they buy. But VDCI's annual client retention rate is outstanding, and almost all of its revenue is recurring. One reason is that its typical municipal government customer pays $250,000 per year for its services—a small amount for most city and county governments. Consequently, the governments often prefer to sign multiyear subscriptions and not deal with the work of an annual renewal process, especially since programs are typically customized and hard to compare, without the promise of substantial savings either way. Of course, for some rural communities, VDCI's services can be a significant portion of the municipal budget. For them, VDCI's high level of service and reliability is important, and leads to a high retention rate. VDCI's service is very specialized and technical. After all, the company is spraying chemicals among voters. You can be sure that the municipal employees who award this contract are very aware that VDCI has done reliable work for their city in prior years.

Being a relatively unimportant part of your customers' total cost structure won't eliminate all price pressure, but it will go a long way toward making you less visible when your customers turn their attention to reducing expenses. That's especially true if you're also competing on your reputation as a high-quality, reliable provider of services: When your service is a small part of your customers' costs but is important enough that they want it done right, nobody wants to be the one who picked a lower-cost provider if something goes wrong. This combination again leads to long-term, enduring profitability. As you examine your target, assess what part its services play in the budgets of its customers to gauge how likely those customers would be to bolt.

Integrating with Customers

Have you ever wondered why your bank offers you a free or an inexpensive electronic bill payment service? It's partly because banks are trying to make it more difficult for you to switch. Before you move to a new bank, you're going to think about painstakingly reentering the information about each company you now pay with the click of a button. This electronic service is much more useful to you than paper check writing, but it also makes you more "sticky" for the bank.

You want to buy a small business whose customers would have to work hard to switch suppliers. A great example is ADEX Machining Technologies, a specialty machine tool shop in South Carolina. It was founded in 1987 as the M. C. Tool Company and, for many years, produced parts for a variety of manufactured products. This was a difficult, competitive business because customers were skillful at using competing machine shops to bargain down prices and raise quality requirements. The business *wasn't* enduringly profitable.

Sean Witty and Jason Premo, who bought the company in 2007, had the idea of gradually shifting to supplying parts for mechanical systems in jet airplanes. This approach was important because in addition to testing and approving the mechanical systems that airplane manufacturers like Boeing buy, the manufacturers also test and approve the parts that their suppliers buy and put into those systems. It is a long, difficult process, and a single component can take a couple of years to get approved. But once an ADEX component is approved by a final assembler like Boeing, it becomes harder for Boeing to switch ADEX out. As a result, ADEX becomes an enduringly profitable business with recurring customers. Sean and Jason took a risk buying a company that was not yet enduringly profitable, but they had a solid plan for moving in that direction after purchase. We'll talk more about this approach later in the chapter.

Sometimes the switching costs just flow naturally from the business's activities. Nurse Care of North Carolina (NNC) is an example of a smaller firm with recurring revenues that support sustainable profits. As described earlier, Ari Medoff conducted a self-funded, regional search that primarily relied on direct sourcing. NNC provides home health-care aides to elderly and disabled people in the Greensboro, North Carolina, area. The company serves 120 to 150 clients who have been referred to NNC by their health-care professionals. Clients pay NNC for each week of service, which is typically provided to a client for months or years. As the home care continues, a rhythm develops, and the relationship formed between the provider and the patient would be difficult to upset. A change might occur if the quality of care is unsatisfactory, but NNC makes sure that never happens. The owner of NNC also concentrates on maintaining excellent relationships with patient referrers—doctors, hospitals, and others—and once a patient selects NNC, they contribute a steady, recurring revenue stream.

NNC's recurring revenue stream contributes to the sustainability of the company's profits in several ways. First, because NNC can project its revenues several months ahead, it can accurately adjust its operating expenses according to this demand. Second, it's tough for competitors to poach clients. Once NNC begins to work with clients, they just aren't in the market for other health-care providers. Finally, NNC's sources of new patients are recurring sources. For example, the geriatric care manager at a local hospital refers patients to NNC month after month because, over the years, patients have reported back that they are well taken care of by the company. Referrers like this aren't interested in experimenting with other services, because satisfied outpatients help their business. Nor is a competitor that offers a price cut likely to win away these referrals—the hospital and its geriatric care manager don't pay for NNC's service; their outpatients do. The referrers are focused on excellent service with no mistakes.

Businesses Without Enduring Profitability

Companies whose profits are less likely to endure also share some common traits:

- **Technology-driven companies:** As the technology changes, so will your customers. You'll need to reinvent their products and find new customers frequently. If you like recurring revenue as we do, you'll steer clear of these companies.

- **Cyclical businesses:** If your customers are able to defer purchasing from you when their business gets soft, your revenues will drop like a stone. Because you will be responsible for regular payments on your acquisition debt, this volatility creates a big problem.

- **Huge competitors:** Avoid any business that a large national chain could compete with. Dance with a giant, and you'll get crushed.

- **Specialized assets:** Avoid any business that requires you to buy specialized equipment that can only be used by one customer. Once you acquire the equipment and the debt that goes with it, the customer can use your weak position to drive prices down.

While we strongly recommend that you focus on enduringly profitable prospects, some searchers have had great success deliberately buying businesses that are initially not enduringly profitable. For example, Sean Witty and Jason Premo bought the manufacturer ADEX before it became enduringly profitable. Another example is Greg Mazur, who purchased a pet food distributor after graduating from Harvard Business School. The company had no exclusive distributorships, and manufacturers and customers could easily switch from one distributor to another, squeezing margins from both directions. He took a business that wasn't enduringly profitable and transformed it into one that was by shifting product lines and growing it into a very successful company selling exclusive, specialty products to the same retailers year after year. Just like start-ups and turnarounds, we believe businesses that are not enduringly profitable are riskier for the buyer and more difficult to manage and require transformation to be successful. That doesn't mean it isn't possible, but we prefer safe and easy to risky and difficult.

Filtering for Enduringly Profitable Prospects

In this chapter, we've focused on the traits we often see in a prospect that has enduring profitability. Ask these important questions about your prospect:

- Does it have a strong reputation?

- Does it lack competitors?

- Is it a small part of its customers' costs and an essential input to the customers' success?

- Is it integrated with its customers?

You might have noticed that almost every example we discussed in this chapter had more than one trait that kept its customers buying year after year. Castronics had a transportation cost advantage, but also had licenses and certification for the products its customers wanted. Vector Disease Control was an unimportant part of the total costs, but also had a reputation for safe and reliable service. ADEX and Nurse Care became enmeshed with their customers and had strong reputations. We think these traits are typical. They are something you should look for in prospects, and the traits should be relatively easy to see early in your filtering. We believe that especially in combination, these traits will lead to enduring profitability with long-lasting, higher margins.

Let's turn back to Randy Shayler to see how these filters applied to the business he was evaluating, Zeswitz Music. Using the information in the CIM to assess the enduring profitability of Zeswitz, Randy found that the company had several of the traits highlighted in this chapter. Zeswitz had a great reputation with the schools it worked with, and its brand name was well established. Indeed, of the 48 school districts that the company did business with, 38 had been with Zeswitz for 20 years or more and were responsible for about 95% of the company's instrumental rentals. Furthermore, the company maintained close ties with the music programs of its schools, handling repairs and replacements of broken instruments quickly and providing other services that integrated Zeswitz with those programs. Instrument rental was also generally a small part of the commitment a parent would make to a child's education so that once a student began renting from Zeswitz, there was little incentive to switch rental companies as long as parents were satisfied with the service they received. While the CIM did not provide specific information about the recurrence of customers, there were strong reasons to conclude that Zeswitz would be an enduringly profitable business.

Next Steps

The initial filters and your qualitative assessment of enduring profitability should enable you to quickly eliminate many business prospects. For those that survive your scrutiny, the next deeper filter is some simple quantitative assessment of enduring profitability, as we describe in the next chapter.

CHAPTER 11

Using Financial Information to Gauge Enduring Profitability

In this chapter, we will show you how to look at several financial measures of a business to *quantitatively* filter your prospects for enduring profitability. Most businesses, even small ones, keep accounting records that can be used to inform these calculations and measures; these should be provided to you after you sign a nondisclosure agreement with the broker or owner. Sometimes this information is kept by a bookkeeper, sometimes by the owner, and sometimes by a professional accountant. For now, assume that the financial information is collected accurately; we'll talk more about how to verify this in chapter 14, "How Much Should You Pay for a Small Business?"

At this filtering stage, you want to spend no more than a day on any one company that survived the initial and deeper qualitative filters. And you should only use the materials you have quickly available to examine the quantitative filters we describe in this chapter.

Earnings Before Interest, Taxes, Depreciation, and Amortization (EBITDA) Margin

Our financial tests begin with a measure of profitability called *EBITDA* (earnings before interest, taxes, depreciation, and amortization). EBITDA and revenue are the most basic pieces of financial information you will learn about a company. If you source through brokers, sales and EBITDA are always provided in the teaser and CIM; if you direct source, these two figures are part of the basic financial information that the owner will share with you as soon as you sign a nondisclosure agreement. *EBITDA margin* is simply EBITDA divided by revenue.

EBITDA margin tells you about the profitability of each dollar of sales and is a good initial test, for two reasons. First, this margin shows that the business is profitable, a central characteristic of enduringly profitable businesses. Second, as we discussed in chapter 10, "Enduringly Profitable Small Businesses," we are looking for small businesses that serve some niche that either keeps others from entering the business or discourages customers from shopping elsewhere. Both increased competition and decreasing customer base, of course, squeeze down EBITDA margins. If a prospect steadily earns a superior EBITDA margin, that's a clue that it possesses some critical quality that keeps competitors and customers from pushing down the margin. Look for large EBITDA margins of at least 20% for manufacturing and service businesses and 15% for higher-volume businesses like wholesalers and distributors. The small-company acquisitions that we describe in this book, for example, have EBITDA margins ranging from 20% to 50%. Margins at this level show that the business is attractively profitable.

The EBITDA margin is very easy to calculate. Just divide the EBITDA by the revenue:

$$EBITDA\ margin = \frac{EBITDA}{Sales} \geq \begin{cases} 20\%\ for\ services\ and \\ manufacturing \\ 15\%\ for\ distribution \\ and\ wholesale \end{cases}$$

Revenue

You already looked at an overall annual revenue number to make sure that the size of the company fits your requirements. Examining several other aspects of revenue records can help confirm that the company's profitability will remain steady. As you move ahead with your investigation of the company, dig into the following questions.

Does this business have recurring revenues? Do the same customers purchase from the prospect again and again? In chapter 10, we looked at indirect indicators of recurring customers, but once you have access to sales records, you can check this directly. The company's *churn rate* is the percentage of customers that buy in one year but not in the next. So, if a company's average churn rate is 5%, it means that each year, 95% of its customers buy again in the following year, which would be outstanding retention. We suggest looking for businesses with churn rates of 25% or less. If the broker or seller has not calculated the business's churn rate, you can calculate it from a customer list by just counting the names that drop off the list each year.

Do the company's top five customers account for a lot of its revenues? The amount of revenue from top customers is called *customer concentration.* High customer concentration—if one customer provides, say, 40% of revenues, or three customers provide 70% of revenues—is a substantial risk to enduring profitability because those important customers have a significant impact on the fortunes of the company.

Is year-to-year sales growth coming from the right places? If you believe that the company's customers are sticky, then most of the business's revenue increases should be coming from market growth, price increases, or new product introductions rather than new customers won from competitors—because it should be hard to poach customers in this industry. If revenue growth is substantial and is coming from new customers won from competitors, or from just one or two customers, you need to look again at the company's recurring revenue or its customer concentration.

Are sales cyclical? The same dip in sales that was merely disruptive for the business's former owner—who has likely operated the company without any debt—may be fatal for you, who will have a considerable amount of borrowed money to return. Examine revenues in 2008 and 2009, the last very deep recession, to see a worst-case scenario. If EBITDA dropped 30% or more, this should be a deal breaker.

Quantitative Filters

In this chapter, we have added some quantitative filters to help you assess the enduring profitability of a prospect:

- ☐ Does it have a high EBITDA margin?

- ☐ Does it have recurring customers?

- ☐ Does it have fragmented customers and suppliers (no concentration)?

- ☐ Does revenue growth come from the right places?

- ☐ Does it have steady sales (not cyclical)?

Returning to Randy Shayler's analysis of Zeswitz Music, he found that the company's EBITDA margin in 2011 was almost 45%, which was very impressive. Most of the sales came from rentals, and the CIM indicated that those relationships with the schools recurred year after year. The CIM also contained information on customer and supplier concentration, and neither was a concern. The growth in rental revenues was slow and seemed to come from the relationships with school districts that were dissatisfied with their current vendor; the revenue from existing relationships was steady because the student population and the proportion participating in music programs with the schools was more or less constant. The long-term financial information provided in the CIM confirmed Randy's expectation that the business was not cyclical and did not suffer a substantial reduction in rentals during the recession. Overall, his analysis convinced him that Zeswitz was an enduringly profitable business.

Next Steps

Zeswitz, like any other company that met a searcher's initial filters and the deeper filter of enduring profitability, has to pass only one additional deeper filter before it survives the filtering stage and moves to preliminary due diligence. Remember, though, that filtering is iterative: As you learn more during the preliminary due-diligence stage, you'll likely update your earlier conclusions, especially your assessment of enduring profitability. But now, we move on to the remaining deeper filter—the owner's commitment to sell—a topic covered in the next chapter.

CHAPTER 12

Filtering for the Owner's Commitment to Sell

The remaining deeper filter is the owner's commitment to sell. You might reasonably wonder why we include this as a filter: Isn't the fact that the owner has retained a broker or, in the case of a directly sourced prospect, engaged in several conversations with you and sent you confidential information a sufficient indication that the owner is a committed seller?

Our experience is that because most owners of the kinds of small businesses we have described are first-time sellers, they aren't yet aware of the consequences of selling their companies. As they learn more during the sales process, they often are disappointed with how hard it is, how long they will have to stay involved in their businesses after the sale, and how little money they get for their companies. Add the owners' commitment to their employees and that their work has defined their lives for decades, and it isn't surprising that many owners who initially are interested in selling decide against it once they are faced with the realities of the process.

But it often takes owners months of learning before they decide to abandon a sale. In the meantime, you are busy working to bring the acquisition to a close, and as we explain in part IV, "Making an Offer," this effort will absorb an enormous amount of your time and substantial cash outlays to lawyers and accountants. When the owner decides not to sell late in the process, it is a miserable experience that could have a devastating impact on your search, especially if you have stopped sourcing new prospects or reached the end of your resources—even if you provided for broken-deal costs in your budgeting, as we recommended earlier.

We suggest applying a filter to gauge the owner's commitment to sell before proceeding to the next stage of your investigation of the company, even if the prospect has passed all your other filters. Like the other deeper filter—enduring profitability—assessing the commitment to sell is an iterative process. As you learn more about the company, you will have a better understanding of why the owner is selling and will therefore (hopefully) be more confident in the owner's commitment to sell.

External Factors

Our experience is that most owners of high-quality smaller firms sell because they have to, not because they want to. Correspondingly, the clearest and most reliable indicator that an owner is committed to selling is an external factor that is compelling the sale. Indeed, that is often the only information you will have about their commitment to sell if your filtering is based on the limited information in a CIM or shared by the owner in a call or two—and it may be very vague. Still, we believe you can glean some real sense of that commitment if one of these situations—or something like them—is forcing the sale:

- Retirement

- Poor health

- Divorce

- Inability of business partners to get along

- Death of the owner, and sale of the business through the estate

Focusing on owners who are experiencing one of these unhappy events doesn't mean you are taking advantage of someone's misfortune. It just means you are looking for sellers who are seriously intending to sell, just as you are seriously intending to buy. Without you—a willing and able buyer—the sellers' choices are much worse.

Most of the entrepreneurs through acquisition that you have met in this book purchased from sellers who faced some sort of compulsion to sell. Greg Ambrosia— the army veteran who purchased the high-rise window-washing business in Dallas—bought the company from two sisters who both wanted to retire and who felt increasing pressure to care for their elderly parents. Family health issues also drove the sale of the fire-hose testing business that Tony Bautista purchased. More recently, one of our students, Eric Calderon, purchased a business that manufactured specialized oil-testing centrifuges. The owner had managed the business until he was 89 years old and in failing health; he died a few months after the transaction was completed.

As Randy Shayler investigated Zeswitz Music, he found no specific compulsion for the owner to sell, but there were, nevertheless, strong indications that the owner was committed to selling the business. The owner also owned a larger company located in New York and New England. The larger company was similar to Zeswitz; the initial intent when Zeswitz was acquired in 2006 had been to combine the operations of the two entities. However, that never happened, and Zeswitz had remained largely a stand-alone business with its own operations and general manager.

Because the CIM didn't specifically address the owner's reason for selling, Randy asked the broker and learned that the owner had abandoned the idea of combining Zeswitz with her larger rental business. She wanted to focus her efforts on the larger business, together with a few other smaller music-related endeavors. This reasoning made sense to Randy, and he moved forward to the preliminary due-diligence stage. Still, he recognized that the owner did not have a compulsion to sell and that she could abandon the sales process later on. In fact, during some tense negotiations, the owner raised the possibility that she would postpone the sale for a few years. This option was never pursued, but, without a compulsion, the risk that a seller might abandon the sale is always present.

Filtering for Commitment to Sell in the Absence of External Factors

Not all owners of high-quality small businesses sell them because of an external compulsion, however. During your search, you will come across owners with all sorts of reasons for selling. Some owners are healthy and energetic but just want to take a break from the constant demands of running a company. Maybe the value of the business has hit their magic number and they want to cash in on their success. Others want to focus their time on a different business, their families, a charitable cause, or a hobby. Business owners certainly sell companies for these reasons, but you need to recognize that owners selling for these reasons can change their minds at any time in the sales process. The filtering challenge is to decide which of the owners who do not have a compulsion to sell are likely to remain committed to the sale through closing.

At the same time, keep an eye out for eager sellers who seem very committed to the sale and who may be hiding a bad deal. We especially distrust owners who tell buyers they are selling because they've taken the business as far as they can and that they believe a new owner can take the business "to the next level." Their statement may be true, but few people, especially those who have managed a business for a decade a more, have such a humble and detached perspective. Still, even if the seller imagines some bad news on the horizon, it could well be a mirage. It is up to you, the buyer, to decide for yourself.

Assessing the owner's commitment to sell when there is no external compulsion to do so is a qualitative process. You are trying to understand whether, later in the process, the owner will learn something that will lead them to abandon the transaction. These triggers often involve disappointment about the owner's cash proceeds from a sale and can stem from various circumstances:

- Differences between presale and postsale after-tax cash flow

- Overestimates of the sales price

- Misunderstanding of the transaction

- Continuing involvement in the business after the sale

We describe each of these traps below, along with ways to filter out or overcome them.

Cash flow consequences for sellers

In chapter 2, "Is Entrepreneurship Through Acquisition for You?," we explained the financial attractiveness of becoming an entrepreneur through acquisition. Of course, if it is financially attractive for the buyer, it is financially unattractive for a seller without external motivation. We emphasized that the acquisition price of a small company is much lower than that of larger, public companies in similar businesses; small firms of the size we discuss in this book regularly sell for three to five times the company's annual profits. That means if an owner is taking home $1.0 million a year in pretax annual profits (which comes out to $600,000 after taxes if the tax rate is 40%), the company is worth somewhere between $3.0 million and $5.0 million. Let's assume a midpoint of $4.0 million. If the owner has to pay capital gains tax of roughly 20% on the sale, the net after-tax proceeds are $3.2 million. If that money is invested in mutual funds, a 10% expected return is probably generous, so the pretax earnings of the seller's portfolio is $320,000. And, of course, income tax is due on those earnings. If the tax rate is 40% on the investment income, the seller's after-tax income is $192,000. That's less than a third of the $600,000 in after-tax income the owner got while running the business. And it might be much less if the owner used the business to shelter some of the income. So, selling is financially very unattractive compared with the annual cash flows from running the business.

Many owners come to understand this arithmetic only late in the selling process. Typically, they will seek some tax advice about how to structure the details of the transaction when there are just a few weeks until the scheduled closing. Some owners still pursue a sale, but others decide to continue to manage the business for a few more years instead of selling immediately. The arithmetic will still be the same when the sale occurs, of course, but the owners can use those years to accumulate more savings, which will allow them to fund their retirement more fully. Others might decide not to sell and instead hire a general manager to run the day-to-day operations of the business for, say, an annual salary of $150,000.

If that works—and it often doesn't—the profitability is reduced from $1.0 million to $850,000, but the owner can retire with much more money than if the business was sold outright and the proceeds invested in mutual funds. Keeping the tax rates in the earlier example, with the manager running the business, the after-tax income of the owner is $510,000 (60% of $850,000), which is much better than $192,000.

As you try to filter on the commitment to sell, seek to gauge whether there is an employee who could be successful as the general manager for an absentee owner; if so, you should be more concerned about the commitment to sell. In contrast, if the owner seems particularly eager to leave the business, perhaps fatigued by the constant demands of the day-to-day management of the business, and there is no competent general manager, you can be more sanguine that the owner will remain committed to selling.

Unrealistic price expectations

Owners who retain brokers or respond favorably to a direct outreach from a searcher may enter the search process even though they are unwilling sell at the prevailing market price for smaller firms. Instead, some might be willing to sell "at the right price." This right price is, of course, a very high price, one you ought to be unwilling to overpay no matter how much you like the business. Other owners are just wondering what their business is worth. That is a natural curiosity because their business is probably their most valuable asset. We think most of these owners, however, are simply unaware of prevailing market conditions and thus substantially overestimate the likely acquisition price for their company.

Because most small business owners are first-time sellers, they often know little about purchase prices of smaller firms. Sale valuations aren't tracked and widely published, so it is very difficult for owners to discover the prices at which similar companies have sold. Imagine trying to keep track of your weight if you never have access to a scale. As the years go by, your own fond self-evaluation gradually drifts away from reality. And in business valuations, both casual acquaintances and market professionals often distort the little market information that is available. Boasting often leads other sellers to express high multiples by underestimating EBITDA and overestimating sale price. Brokers, in an attempt to portray their abilities to potential clients, also do much the same.

Furthermore, owners preparing for a sale often reconstruct their business's financials incorrectly. For example, they may add back to their company's profit the salary they receive and not recognize that after they sell, the business will still have to pay a CEO's salary, though it will be paid to someone else. Sometimes, owners set their business's valuation multiple by comparing it to a large publicly traded company in a similar industry, not understanding that the multiples for smaller companies are much smaller. Sometimes, owners decide on their selling price by imagining the amount of money they want to have in retirement, rather than reflecting the economics of the business. Owners might seek advice, but it often comes from a family attorney or a tax accountant who has little exposure to the market prices for smaller firms.

Most owners learn about the true value of their business during the sales process, and first-time sellers are almost always disappointed.

As a result, an owner's initial interest in selling isn't a reliable indication that he or she has a sense of the prevailing market prices for smaller companies. To filter out this unreliability, talk to the broker, if there is one. Ask about the price expectations of the seller as one of your follow-up questions on a CIM. The seller's opening number will obviously be on the higher end of the negotiating range, but if it is 5x the EBITDA, you'll know that the owner is more committed than if the broker tells you the number is 10x this figure.

For directly sourced prospects, it is trickier because you won't know much about the business during your first few conversations with the owner. But you can still suggest a general valuation range: "I'm looking to buy a business at 3x–5x pretax EBITDA." The response should help you gauge whether the owner's idea of the purchase price is within the prevailing market range and thus whether the owner will remain committed to selling at that range. It is essential that, early on, you filter out the owners who have unreasonable price expectations; you cannot waste time pursuing a deal that will never occur.

Misunderstanding the sales process

There are two common deal terms that often confuse owners and cause them to abandon the acquisition late in the process. The first is that small businesses are purchased on a *debt-free and cash-free* basis, and the second is that these deals typically include a so-called normal amount of working capital. Both of these terms are explained in detail in the asset purchase agreement, which is negotiated by lawyers late in the sales process, so disagreements over these two terms arise late. Moreover, because the amounts of money involved can be substantial, these disagreements often mean the abandonment of the deal. We'll explain each of the terms in more detail in part V, "Completing the Acquisition," but we'll sketch out the issues here to give you a sense of how to filter for the owner's commitment to sell.

A debt-free, cash-free acquisition means that the seller gets to keep the cash in the business but also must pay any outstanding debt of the business. So, if there is a $500,000 cash balance in the business's bank account, the seller gets to keep that money at the closing. The seller will think that fair because the business earned that money while he or she managed it. But if there is a $1.0 million loan, perhaps related to the purchase of a building or a piece of machinery, the seller needs to pay off that loan; the buyer doesn't have this liability, even though the buyer gets the building or the machine the borrowed money was used to purchase. Some sellers misunderstand this term, and one very disappointed searcher reported that a seller abandoned an acquisition within a few weeks of the scheduled close even after multiple discussions about pricing. As the seller told the searcher, "I thought those pricing discussions were about my equity and that you were going to assume all the debt. After all, you are getting the assets; it makes sense you should get the debt too."

Working capital is the amount of money needed to run the business. Most simply, it is accounts receivable plus inventory minus accounts payable. Sometimes there are other items too. When you agree on a price—a topic covered in part IV, "Making an Offer"—you specify an amount of working capital that will stay with the business. In many small businesses, this amount is substantial, sometimes in the millions of dollars, but more often in the hundreds of thousands. The buyer includes the working capital because it is, effectively, an operating asset of the business. The seller, however, has a different view, and deals often break down over this issue. As sellers explain it, "Those sales were made when I owned the business, so I should get that revenue when it is eventually paid. The accounts receivable should be mine."

To filter out these misunderstandings, we recommend that you talk with the owner about these terms repeatedly throughout the sales process, certainly beginning no later than when you submit your first offer. You can also, earlier on, get a sense of what the owner understands would "go with" the business. It can be an informal conversation, but it should give you a good idea of whether the owner understands these deal terms and considered them in the transaction price.

Continuing involvement after the sale

Owners generally believe that when they sell their businesses, they get the purchase price in cash, are completely finished with the business, and then move on to whatever they plan to do next. In fact, it rarely works that way. Typically, the seller needs to continue working with the buyer for three to six months after the purchase to help with the management transition. These owners keep a lot of the information about the business—customer preferences and promises, for example—in their heads, and the buyer's only mechanism to reliably learn that information is for the seller to help "train" the buyer.

Plus, as we will explain later, sellers typically lend the buyer part of the purchase price. Part of the purchase price is also usually tied up in escrow accounts, and some of it might be in the form of an *earn-out,* in which the seller gets some portion of future profits. So, the seller needs to stay involved and the searcher needs to filter the search for the owner's willingness to work with the buyer for some period after the transaction is completed and to help finance the purchase. Again, this filtering is largely qualitative; if the owner cannot seem to interact professionally with you at this early stage, the likelihood of a smooth transition after an eventual sale is far less. Similarly, if the owner has plans—"I've been getting my boat ready to sail around the world"—be dubious about the transition and the willingness to help finance the transaction.

Are *All* Owners Committed to Selling?

As you investigate an owner's willingness to sell, don't forget that, sometimes, ownership is held by more than one partner and only one partner is committed to selling. For example, a business we observed had been started by three partners. Now, one partner was in ill health and ready to sell, while the other two were in fine health, happy to keep working, but willing to sell at "the right price." Of course, all of the discussions around the sale occurred with the partner who had a compelling reason to sell, and the deal seemed to be moving along at reasonable market terms—until the other two partners rejected the deal late in the process. In another instance, a potential seller gave away small ownership percentages to key employees as he slowly disengaged from the day-to-day operations. The seller thought he could convince the minority holders to sell, but he could not and the deal collapsed.

As you search, filter on ownership structure. The more complex the structure, the less likely it is that *all* the owners will be committed sellers.

Next Steps

The trick to efficiently managing your search is to be ruthless and quick in rejecting prospects by applying the initial and deeper filters we've discussed in this part of the book. If a prospect has passed these filters, you'll move on to preliminary due diligence.

But remember, it is an iterative process in two ways. First, you'll always be going back over your filters, especially the deeper filters on enduring profitability and the owner's commitment to sell, throughout the sales process as you learn more information.

Second, what you learn in the filtering stage will have an impact on your upcoming due diligence. We think you should be especially cautious of young, healthy sellers who face no external compulsion to sell. No matter how much investigation you do, the sellers will always know the business better than you will. You will need to work especially hard during the due-diligence stage to make sure they aren't unloading the business before some bad news becomes apparent, and hopefully your diligent investigation will uncover any problems.

PART FOUR

Making an Offer

You seem to have found the small business that you have been searching for, one that has survived all of your filters. But before you make an offer to buy the company, you need to learn more about it to determine if the prospect is, in fact, a good acquisition candidate. We describe this process in **chapter 13, "Preliminary Due Diligence."** If you decide to pursue the prospect after completing preliminary due diligence, you'll need to determine a reasonable offer price and other acquisition terms. We provide guidance on pricing in **chapter 14, "How Much Should You Pay for a Small Business?,"** and other terms in **chapter 15, "Deal Terms."** These come together in a formal offer, called a letter of intent, which we cover in **chapter 16, "The Offer."**

CHAPTER 13

Preliminary Due Diligence

Once a prospect survives your filters, it is time to learn even more about it so that you can decide whether to make an offer to buy the company in the form of a letter of intent (LOI)—and determine what shape the offer will take. Gathering the information to apply your filters probably took about a day's work and, for prospects sourced through brokers, included an initial discussion with the broker after reading the teaser and CIM and, for directly sourced prospects, included interviewing the owner and reading company financials. Now, you'll devote substantially more time to the prospect in the focused period of rapid learning, your *preliminary due diligence*. The goal of preliminary due diligence is not to learn how to operate the business; it is to efficiently get to a go/no-go decision and to shape the price and terms of your offer.

Much as with filtering, you'll begin by focusing on potential concerns that would cause you to reject the prospect. Unlike filtering, the characteristics you will focus on are likely to be less visible and will require that you reach beyond the teaser and the CIM, requesting additional pieces of information from the broker and perhaps the seller and doing your own projections and analysis. While the filtering process is about running a prospect through a static checklist of filters, preliminary due diligence is about formulating and then answering questions very specific to a particular business to get a more detailed sense of how it operates.

To minimize costs, you will do almost all the preliminary due diligence yourself. You'll begin to bring in accountants and attorneys only after you become even surer that this is a good opportunity.

The Questions

Preliminary due diligence is about forming and answering questions. The time you invest in formulating thoughtful questions makes the process more efficient. Consider unknowns that are essential to the company's business model. Ask yourself, What are the two or three things that would change my mind about the business? Remember, it is an iterative process so that many of the questions you focus on during this stage will be the same as those you examined during filtering. But now, you are looking to answer those questions more fully and to be more confident in your answers. So, as you create your list of the two or three most important things to focus on, also ask, How can I satisfy my concerns? What data can I ask for? What could I ask the owner? Each business is different, and you will have different questions about every one that you investigate. Here are some examples:

- I *think* the business has many recurring customers. But does it? What is the history of customer churn?

- I *think* the business has good growth potential because the current owner hasn't done much selling. But is the growth potential real? How big is the market? How would the business compete for new customers?

- I *think* the business has been enduringly profitable with steady cash flows. But has it? What were its profits and cash flows during the last recession? Is it cyclical?

- I *think* the business does not rely on particular customers, suppliers, or employees. But does it? What is the customer concentration? What is the supplier concentration? Are there key employees?

- I *think* I can run this business at least as well as the seller can. But can I? Are there some key relationships between the seller and customers or suppliers? Is there some certification or expertise required? Do I need a license? Is there a preference for an attribute (veteran, women, and underrepresented minority) that I lack?

Whatever your questions, order them so that you first focus on the ones most likely to kill the deal. Preliminary due diligence is an iterative process; as you obtain answers, new questions get raised. So, as you formulate your additional questions, keep focused on those that could influence your decision to move forward or not.

As you proceed with your investigation, you will use resources beyond those that you used to filter and you will probe deeper into the resources you've already used.

Reading Industry Research

To learn more about broad industry trends, terminology, and rules of thumb, turn to industry research. Search the web for news stories, and read trade publications and analyst reports on any large public companies in the sector. Industry associations often offer a library of reference materials. Internet searches are fast ways to gather background information. As you investigate, gauge whether the industry is growing or is mature and whether there are emerging, competitive threats.

You are unlikely to find information that is precisely applicable to the prospect you are evaluating, because most successful smaller firms operate within narrow, differentiated niches. Still, this background information will give you a context in which to evaluate the acquisition and prepare you for your conversations with the seller. In addition, understanding the industry and who the competition is (or isn't) can help you confirm your assumptions about the company's business model.

Interviewing the Seller

The simplest way to get your questions answered is to arrange a telephone interview with the owner and go through your questions. This detailed call might last one or two hours and may include requests by you for additional information. Such a phone call works well for questions that can be answered quantitatively. If your concern is about cyclicity, for example, the owner can send the company's financial results from the last recession. Similarly, the owner can provide more detailed information about customer churn and concentration. Interviewing the seller is also helpful with qualitative questions such as why customers buy from the company or its closest competitors. Of course, the owner will be optimistic about the prospect, as any seller would be. The challenge for you is to listen and then carefully assess the answers afterward; it is not a time for an adversarial call.

You may be tempted to visit the owner in person for this first in-depth interview, but a call is actually more productive and less expensive. The seller is unlikely to be able to answer your quantitative questions during an on-site visit anyway; just as with a phone call, you'll need to wait to get that data afterward. In addition, at this point you don't want to convey to the seller that you are overly eager.

Conducting an Onsite Visit

An onsite visit does make sense later in your preliminary due diligence, however, after your most critical questions have been answered favorably. As the chance of completing an acquisition increases, the additional investment of your time and funds makes more sense. Certainly, most owners will also want to have met their buyer in person before accepting any kind of offer or letter of intent, so you should plan to visit as you get closer to finalizing your offer.

At an onsite visit, you usually have the opportunity to talk directly with the owner about the business and its challenges and opportunities. The visit works best if it is a free-flowing conversation in which you learn a lot about the business that goes beyond the initial information you received while filtering. The conversation will sharpen your understanding of how the business operates. How are its products manufactured? Who are its important suppliers? Why do customers choose to buy from this company and not from its competitors? Which employees are the most valuable, and why?

Once you are onsite, not only can you meet with the seller, but you can also observe the business in action. You can learn about the facilities from seeing them operate and from observing the property. Is the facility neat and professional? Are employees busy and hard at work? Is there room for expansion if needed? Is the production process orderly, or is there a constant sense of confusion?

You will also learn more about the seller. You'll get a feel for the seller's capability and integrity. You'll glean more information about the owner's commitment to sell the business and the ease of the postsale transition by observing how involved the seller is in the day-to-day operation of the business. Importantly, you will also discover if the two of you will be able to develop a mutually satisfactory relationship.

One thing that won't happen during an initial onsite visit is a meeting with the management team. Sellers typically keep a sale process quiet until it is more certain. Sometimes, sellers might want to meet with you on weekends or evenings so that the onsite meeting happens without the knowledge of the management team.

Other times, you might not be introduced fully or at all. The seller isn't being rude; he or she is just being understandably secretive about the impending sale.

Building a Financial Projection

A financial projection is a numerical expression of your evolving beliefs about the business and how it will perform over time, depending on any changes that you decide to make. The projection should reflect your estimates for revenues, expenses, and EBITDA, typically over five years. You will return to the financial model repeatedly throughout your preliminary due diligence and beyond. As you learn more about the prospect, you'll incorporate that information into the model so that you can gauge the financial consequences of your increased understanding about the business.

To give you a concrete example, we will apply the use of a financial projection to Randy Shayler's acquisition of Zeswitz Music. (We have changed some details to protect Randy's privacy and that of the seller and to make the example clearer.) As described earlier, Zeswitz rents musical instruments to schoolchildren. Excerpts from the teaser for the prospect were presented in chapter 8, "Sourcing Prospects Using Brokers," and Randy's filtering process was described throughout part III, "Finding the Right Small Business to Buy."

Generally, you'll begin your financial model by examining the financial information you received from the broker in the CIM or from the seller for a directly sourced prospect. To do so, create a summary of the business's operating results like the one in table 13-1, listing its revenues, cost of goods sold (COGS), margin, operating

TABLE 13-1

Zeswitz Music, summary of historical operating results

			YEAR ENDING DECEMBER 31		2012
	2008	2009	2010	2011	(projected)
Rentals	2,391	2,480	2,492	2,756	2,808
Retail sales	1,024	932	590	565	575
Lessons	—	—	—	19	76
Total revenue	3,415	3,412	3,082	3,340	3,459
Cost of goods sold (COGS)	791	688	496	526	472
Gross profit	2,624	2,724	2,586	2,814	2,987
Gross margin	77%	80%	84%	84%	86%
Operating expenses					
Advertising	13	4	4	9	9
Auto	57	62	65	48	59
Commissions	45	64	71	59	67
Credit card fees	41	47	50	54	53
Insurance	115	119	98	66	92
Accounting services	36	24	22	21	21
Office expense	30	16	30	15	14
Payroll	1,135	1,095	1,137	869	852
Rent	186	149	109	82	87
Travel & trade shows	9	7	6	4	6
Miscellaneous	48	79	71	72	75
Contract/professional fees	28	0	-2	15	6
Printing & postage	41	42	46	52	51
Other taxes	6	0	3	9	3
Utilities/communications	72	69	65	69	74
Total operating expense	1,862	1,777	1,775	1,444	1,469

EBITDA*	762	947	811	1,370	1,518
Stand-alone EBITDA adjustments					
Extraordinary expenses/legal matter	50	50	50	50	0
Old facility-related other expenses	0	0	12	0	0
Old facility-related legal expenses	0	1	6	4	0
Noncontinuing advisory expenses	0	0	0	0	17
Total stand-alone adjustments	50	51	68	54	17
Adjusted EBITDA	**812**	**998**	**879**	**1,424**	**1,535**
Potential synergy adjustments					
Purchases (10% of total purchases)	50	45	80	43	25
Trade show expenses	5	5	5	5	5
Postage	5	6	36	49	36
Total potential synergy adjustments	60	56	121	97	66
Adjusted EBITDA with pro forma combination synergy savings	**872**	**1,054**	**1,000**	**1,521**	**1,601**
Less capital expenditures	851	401	689	321	200
Free cash flow	**21**	**653**	**311**	**1,200**	**1,401**
Other financial information					
Depreciation	589	546	564	698	720
Interest expense	130	143	82	84	72

Note: Unless marked as a percentage, all numbers are in thousands of dollars.

*EBITDA, earnings before interest, taxes, depreciation, and amortization.

expenses, and other financial data year by year. The financials contained in table 13-1 are from the Zeswitz CIM, which provides detailed financial results for the previous four fiscal years and a projection for the next year. The CIM doesn't provide detail on the components of COGS, but Randy assumed these were largely the cost of the musical instruments that were sold to customers.

Note that in addition to revenues and expenses, the summary contains two sets of adjustments to EBITDA, or so-called *add-backs*. The first set includes expenses that the seller wants the buyer to consider extraordinary. The CIM explains that these were onetime expenses unrelated to the ongoing business. Randy accepted those additions at face value but recognized that he would need to learn more about them if the deal moved forward. The second set of adjustments is the broker's projections of synergies if the company were to be purchased by a larger strategic acquirer; these numbers were irrelevant to Randy because the synergies wouldn't exist in his case, since he would operate Zeswitz as a stand-alone business.

As a second step in building a financial model, you need to analyze the historical results by looking at each key component of the financials (revenue, COGS, gross margin, operating expense, etc.) as a percentage of revenue, creating a document like the one in table 13-2. The first thing to notice is that 2011—the last full year before the company went on the market—was an especially good year for Zeswitz. Every component of cost was at its lowest percentage of sales. The same was true for capital expenditures. If the 2011 results were sustainable, Randy reflected, Zeswitz was a fabulous prospect. But he wondered if assuming that the future would be like the com-

TABLE 13-2

Zeswitz Music, analysis of historical operating results as a percentage of revenue

| | YEAR ENDING DECEMBER 31 | | | | | |
	2008	2009	2010	2011	2012 (projected)	Average
Total revenue	100%	100%	100%	100%	100%	100%
COGS*	23%	20%	16%	16%	14%	18%
Gross margin	77%	80%	84%	84%	86%	82%
Total operating expense	55%	52%	58%	43%	42%	50%
EBITDA margin**	**22%**	**28%**	**26%**	**41%**	**44%**	**32%**
Adjusted EBITDA margin	**24%**	**29%**	**29%**	**43%**	**44%**	**34%**
Capital expenditures	25%	12%	22%	10%	6%	15%
Free cash flow	**–1%**	**17%**	**6%**	**33%**	**39%**	**19%**

*COGS, cost of goods sold.
**EBITDA, earnings before interest, taxes, depreciation, and amortization.

pany's best year would make his projections too optimistic. So, he computed the company's *average* margins (the last column of table 13-2) as well.

Next, use this analysis to create a first pass at projections of how the company will perform in the future (table 13-3). Because he had yet to obtain detailed information about sales to new schools, Randy started with an assumption that total revenue would grow by a modest 5% annually, knowing that he would want to return to that assumption as he learned more. For the other items, he decided line by line whether to use the 2011 results or the average, or something in between. He set the COGS percentage of sales at the 2011 percentage largely because it had been steady at 16% for the last two years. He set the total operating expense as percentage of revenue at 48%; the average was 50% but it was much

TABLE 13-3

Zeswitz Music, financial projections for the next five years

KEY ASSUMPTIONS

Revenue growth rate	5%
COGS as percentage of revenue	16%
Total operating expense as percentage of revenue	48%
Capital expenditures as percentage of revenue	15%

	FOR YEAR ENDING DECEMBER 31					
	2012	**2013**	**2014**	**2015**	**2016**	**2017**
Total revenue	3,459	3,632	3,814	4,005	4,205	4,415
COGS*	472	581	610	641	673	706
Gross profit	2,987	3,051	3,204	3,364	3,532	3,709
Total operating expense less stand-alone adjustments	1,452	1,743	1,831	1,922	2,018	2,119
EBITDA**	**1,535**	**1,308**	**1,373**	**1,442**	**1,514**	**1,590**
Less capital expenditures	200	545	572	601	631	662
Free cash flow	**1,335**	**763**	**801**	**841**	**883**	**928**

Note: Unless marked as a percentage, all numbers are in thousands of dollars.
*COGS, cost of goods sold.
**EBITDA, earnings before interest, taxes, depreciation, and amortization.

lower in 2011 at 43% and was on track for 42% for 2012, so he picked a number in between the average and recent results. He noted that learning more about these expenses would be a key due-diligence item. Finally, he set capital expenditures at the average level of 15% of revenue because he guessed that the swings in yearly expenditures had more to do with the availability of capital than with the needs of the business. Again, he would need to learn more.

As he studied his results, Randy noted that the EBITDA during each year of the projection period except for 2017 was lower than the 2012 result and that free cash flow was much lower than 2012, largely driven by the especially low capital expenditures in 2012. Still, the EBITDA margin (EBITDA/total revenue) was a healthy 36%. So, while Randy's first version of his model raised several questions, he remained optimistic about Zeswitz and therefore continued with the iterative preliminary due diligence to get answers to those questions.

Of course, it's difficult to forecast the future, and the test of a financial model is not that it predicts with exact accuracy. A financial model enables you to play with your key assumptions to see the effects on other parts of the business: For example, if sales increase or decrease, in contrast to your plan, what is the effect on cash flows? Gradually, as you adjust the important assumptions in your forecast, you develop a sense of the likely range of performance of your business. For example, if the 2011 ratios for Zeswitz were sustainable, the financial projections would improve substantially: EBITDA in 2016 would be over $1.7 million, and free cash flow would be $1.3 million. Your financial modeling provides insights on whether the business, as you understand it, is enduringly profitable and then identifies the critical assumptions that you need to explore further during the preliminary due-diligence process.

Next Steps

If your preliminary due diligence—including your initial financial model—reinforces your view that the prospect would be a good acquisition for you, the next step is to determine an offer price and other important terms of your proposed acquisition. We discuss this step in chapter 14, "How Much Should You Pay for a Small Business?," and chapter 15, "Deal Terms."

How Much Should You Pay for a Small Business?

The purchase price of a small business is often expressed as a multiple of the most recent year's EBITDA. The kind of enduringly profitable small business that we've described in this book—with EBITDA of between $750,000 and $2.0 million—tends to be priced between 3 and 5 times the EBITDA (often expressed as "3x–5x"). This means that if the most recent year's EBITDA is $1 million, the purchase price would range from $3.0 million to $5.0 million. While not all smaller businesses sell in this range—distressed firms typically sell for less, and firms that appear to have enormous growth potential often sell for more—our experience and research indicate that this price range does apply to enduringly profitable, smaller firms in traditional industries with established business models and moderate growth prospects. Larger companies often cost much more—more like 6x–12x EBITDA.

Both of searcher and entrepreneur Doren Spinner's two acquisitions, for example, have reflected this market pricing with an eerie precision even though they occurred almost a decade apart. In 2003, Doren acquired the Acken Sign Company in Bluefield, Virginia. This manufacturer of large-scale illuminated signs generated revenues of $6.0 million and an EBITDA of $650,000; Doren and his investor group purchased it for $2.5 million, or 4x EBITDA. He sold the business in 2011, conducted another search, and, in September 2012, acquired Norfil, a Seattle-based aerospace parts manufacturer at roughly the same multiple.

Across the continent from Seattle, Jim Goodman is the founder and president of Gemini Investors, a Massachusetts-based private-equity partnership that invests exclusively in smaller companies. It's an excellent observation post from which to see how smaller firms are bought and sold. The businesses in which Gemini invests are profitable, smaller companies that cut across the US economy: tire distributors, casual restaurant chains, medical service companies, and many others. Over the 20 years since its founding, Jim's firm has invested in about 100 smaller companies and evaluated almost 10,000 opportunities. In describing to his investors the valuations of smaller firms, Jim observed, "The purchase price multiple paid has rarely exceeded 6x, most commonly has been 4x–5x and on (a few) occasions has been below 4x."[1]

It is because these purchase-price multiples are so low, incidentally, that these smaller businesses provide significant financial opportunities for potential buyers. After all, buying a company at a 4x EBITDA—earning, say, $1.0 million of EBITDA annually on a purchase price of $4.0 million—provides a 25% yield on your investment every year. If, as we will recommend, you pay for your new business in part by borrowing against it and in part with equity, your return on equity will be even higher and well above investment returns available elsewhere.

Still, the range of 3x–5x is substantial; as you complete your preliminary due diligence on an attractive prospect, you should begin forming an idea of where in that range your offer should fall. This chapter guides you through several methods you can use to set your offer price.

Adjusting the Multiple

You'll need to base the offer price both on the general range of 3x–5x EBITDA and on factors that make the firm more or less valuable within that range. Such factors include the following:

- **Growth:** A company with increasing EBITDA is worth more than a company with flat or shrinking EBITDA. The faster the growth rate, the higher the multiple.

- **Predictability:** A company with a predictable, reliable EBITDA is worth more than one whose EBITDA is volatile. And the longer the track record of predictability, the better. Predictability enables an owner to more efficiently plan spending levels—a practice that should produce higher profits. In addition, predictability allows owners to borrow with confidence a bit more on their business, and those extra borrowings increase return on equity.

- **Cash flow conversion:** A company that requires significant, ongoing reinvestment in equipment, inventory, or receivables is worth less than one that does not require reinvestment. With a lower need for reinvestment, a company has more cash available to pay off debt or to distribute to shareholders.

- **Size:** Generally, multiples increase as EBITDA increases. In other words, you pay more per dollar of EBITDA for a company earning $2.5 million in EBITDA than for a company earning $0.5 million in EBITDA. This is because a business's size is usually associated with other strengths, such as a broader management team, a more diversified customer and supplier base, and access to more financing options. Moreover, larger companies attract more buyers (such as private-equity firms), and these buyers tend to bid up multiples.

- **Corporate structure:** Pass-through corporations are more tax-efficient than other corporate structures. Prospects that are not structured as pass-through corporations sell at a substantial discount to those that are.

One way to narrow your valuation is to compare the business to others whose prices you know. Unfortunately, few small business sales make their details available, so it is unlikely you'll find a similar company that you can use to benchmark your price. But if you can find comparable transactions to guide your offer, it is usually very helpful because the seller is probably also aware of those transactions and has anchored price expectations to them.

Adjusting EBITDA

As you home in on the right price for your target, make sure that the EBITDA figure you are working with is accurate—that it's unpolluted by extraneous transactions such as personal expenses of the seller or onetime revenues or expenditures. As you review the company's financials and find out about those kinds of transactions, adjust the EBITDA and thus your price accordingly so that they reflect the more normal earnings likely to occur under your initial ownership.

For example, because you will permit the seller to add back personal expenses, you need to remove those expenses from your calculation of EBITDA. As you do, be careful: Sellers often overestimate those personal expenses to improve the business's perceived financial performance. For example, sellers often add back the entirety of their salaries, explaining that they were paying themselves an above-market rate; however, it is only appropriate to add back the portion that is *excess* compensation because you will have to pay yourself a market rate to manage the business.

Also look for nonrecurring business expenses that occurred during the year in question. For example, a company might have spent $100,000 in moving expenses as it began a 10-year lease on new headquarters space. Buyers and sellers often have different views about how much of these nonrecurring business expenses will be added back in computing adjusted EBITDA.

Pricing as a multiple of historical EBITDA implicitly assumes that those earnings will continue in the future. That isn't always true, even for enduringly profitable businesses. A large contract could, perhaps, have only one year remaining, and renewal might be a competitive process. Sometimes, owners decide to sell after a particularly good year. We saw such an example in chapter 13, "Primary Due Diligence," when Randy Shayler analyzed the Zeswitz financials. Other times, owners fabricate good results by deferring costs or accelerating revenues. Whatever the reason, our pricing range assumes that the historical results are predictive of the future; if your investigation suggests otherwise, you need to adjust your measure of EBITDA, which, in turn, will affect your offer price.

Adjusting purchase price for seller debt

The full offer price of the acquisition is rarely paid all at once. A key component of the other terms of the offer, which we will discuss in more detail in the chapter 15, "Deal Terms," is *seller debt*. In a typical seller-debt arrangement, you pay part of the purchase price over several years instead of all at once.

The multiple will change as the form of payment changes; an all-cash offer for the same firm will be at a lower multiple than one with a significant component of seller debt. Such a differential exists because an all-cash deal is less risky to the seller than a seller-debt deal, whose payout is deferred.

Pricing your prospect according to EBITDA multiples is a starting point and a good benchmark for determining if you and the seller have a similar view. Most searchers will use the 3x–5x range of multiples, together with adjustments, to zero in on a reasonable offer price. If the seller shares this view of a reasonable price, it is time to refine your offer by constructing a more detailed model of the prospect.

Using Your Financial Projection to Value Your Business

The best way to value a potential acquisition is to use the financial projections you began constructing during your preliminary due diligence. To do so, continue to build your model to reflect your plans for the business along with the proposed offer price and information on how you plan to finance its acquisition. Then use the model to calculate the expected rate of return, given your assumptions. Test the model with different assumptions to determine which purchase prices will bring you and your investors a reasonable return—and to determine problem areas for further study if your anticipated purchase price range isn't yielding the right rate of return. A normal market return to equity investors in a smaller firm is around 25% annually. Of course, if you can do better, that's great. Also, note that your reward comes *after* the investors earn their return, so the projected return on the cash flows that you and your investors will share would need to be well above the 25%. We will discuss total return targets and the sharing between you and your investors further in chapter 19, "Raising Acquisition Equity."

We'll discuss financing alternatives in later chapters, but for your preliminary financial model, you need to make some financing assumptions. To complete the model, you will also need to assume that you will eventually sell the business. For this assumption, you must decide on a multiple at which the company is sold. It's a prudent idea to set that exit multiple at either the same multiple as, or a multiple less than, the one at which you are acquiring the business. Don't expect that you can buy a business at 4x EBITDA and sell it at 6x EBITDA.

Earlier, we discussed Randy's analysis of Zeswitz's historical results and how he projected the financials for the business over the next five years under his ownership. Now, in the preliminary model shown in table 14-1, we show how to take the projections another step forward by estimating the returns he and his investors would receive from the acquisition, given certain assumptions:

- A purchase price of 4x 2012 EBITDA, 30% funded by bank debt, another 30% in the form of seller debt, and the remaining 40% provided by equity investors

- Acquisition costs—the accountant and attorney, for example—totaling $150,000

- The exit multiple in year 5 is the same as the acquisition multiple (in this case, 4)

All of these assumptions are in line with a typical acquisition of a smaller firm.

TABLE 14-1

Zeswitz Music acquisition financial model, version 1

KEY ASSUMPTIONS

Purchase price as a multiple of 2012 EBITDA ($1,535)*	4
Leverage ratio, bank	30%
Debt rate, bank	6%
Leverage ratio, seller	30%
Debt rate, seller	8%

HYPOTHETICAL ACQUISITION FUNDING

Uses		Sources	
Purchase price	6,140	Bank debt	1,887
Acquisition costs	150	Seller debt	1,887
		Investor equity	2,516
	6,290		6,290

YEAR ENDING DECEMBER 31

	2013	2014	2015	2016	2017
Free cash flow from table 13-3	763	801	841	883	928
Exit (4 x the 2017 EBITDA of $1,590 from table 13-3)					6,360
Bank debt					
Beginning debt	1,887	1,388	821	180	0
Interest on debt	113	83	49	11	0
Debt repayment	499	567	641	180	0
Ending debt	1,388	821	180	0	0
Seller debt					
Beginning debt	1,887	1,887	1,887	1,887	1,346
Interest on debt	151	151	151	151	108
Debt repayment	0	0	0	541	1,346
Ending debt	1,887	1,887	1,887	1,346	0
Available equity cash flow after debt payments	0	0	0	0	5,833
IRR to owner plus equity investors**	18%				

Note: Unless marked as a percentage or a multiple for the purchase price, all numbers are in thousands of dollars.

*EBITDA, earnings before interest, taxes, depreciation, and amortization.

**IRR, internal rate of return.

We begin the preliminary model with the free cash flow projections from table 13-3. We then calculate the outstanding bank debt balance and interest each year, and the same for the seller debt. This model assumes that the bank requires all cash flow not used in the business to be used to repay the bank loan, so that the $499,000 loan repayment in 2013 is just the free cash flow of $763,000 less $113,000 interest on the bank loan and $151,000 interest on the seller loan. Because the bank loan takes five years to pay off, the seller receives only interest and there are no cash flows available after debt payments for the first four years for either Randy or his investors. In year 5, the model imagines a hypothetical sale at the acquisition multiple; the sale provides the funds to repay the remaining debts and leaves about $5.8 million for Randy and his investors.

The last line of table 14-1 shows the *internal rate of return* (IRR) of the available equity cash flows. The IRR of 18% is well below the acceptable range of 25%. If Randy completed the deal with these assumptions, it is unlikely that he could raise equity from investors, because there isn't enough reward for risk and illiquidity inherent in investing in a smaller firm. In addition, Randy himself would not be sufficiently compensated for his time and efforts.

But it's not time to abandon the prospect yet. Looking closely at our history of operating results (refer back to table 13-1), we can see that the reason the IRR is low is that the cash flows are low relative to EBITDA because of the high capital expenditures. Earlier in this chapter, we noted that low cash flow is a reason to reduce the

TABLE 14-2

Zeswitz Music acquisition financial model, version 2, with a reduced purchase and exit multiple

KEY ASSUMPTIONS	
Purchase price as a multiple of 2012 EBITDA ($1,535)*	3
Leverage ratio, bank	30%
Debt rate, bank	6%
Leverage ratio, seller	30%
Debt rate, seller	8%

HYPOTHETICAL ACQUISITION FUNDING

Uses		Sources	
Purchase price	4,605	Bank debt	1,427
Acquisition costs	150	Seller debt	1,427
		Investor equity	1,901
	4,755		4,755

YEAR ENDING DECEMBER 31

	2013	2014	2015	2016	2017
Free cash flow from table 13-3	763	801	841	883	928
Exit (3 x the 2017 EBITDA of $1,590 from table 13-3)					4,770
Bank debt					
Beginning debt	1,427	864	229	0	0
Interest on debt	86	52	14	0	0
Debt repayment	563	635	229	0	0
Ending debt	864	229	0	0	0
Seller debt					
Beginning debt	1,427	1,427	1,427	943	135
Interest on debt	114	114	114	75	11
Debt repayment	0	0	484	808	135
Ending debt	1,427	1,427	943	135	0
Available equity cash flow after debt payments	0	0	0	0	5,551
IRR to owner plus equity investors**	24%				

Note: Unless marked as a percentage or a multiple for the purchase price, all numbers are in thousands of dollars.

*EBITDA, earnings before interest, taxes, depreciation, and amortization.

**IRR, internal rate of return.

offer price below 4x EBITDA. And indeed, table 14-2 shows that the IRR improves to 24% if the acquisition price is reduced to 3x.

However, Randy believed that it was very unlikely that the owner—who, as we have seen, was not compelled to sell—would accept such a low price. Instead, Randy decided to revisit his assumption about the instrument purchases that constituted most of the capital expenditures. If he could substantially reduce the instrument purchases, cash flows would be closer to EBITDA and the deal would be more viable. To test his intuition, he revised his model: again an acquisition cost of 4x EBITDA and capital expenditures reduced by half. As table 14-3 shows, the revision gave him a 25% IRR.

This kind of what-if analysis is the primary function of a model during preliminary due diligence because it points you to the important assumptions about the prospect—aspects that require further study before you can finalize an offer. For Randy's acquisition of Zeswitz, he would need to study the instrument purchases that made up the bulk of the capital expenditures and see if, in fact, he was comfortable that he could run the business with just half of the historical level.

Deciding on an Offer Price Strategy

Once you have narrowed down the price that you are willing to pay, you'll need to decide whether to bid the highest price and the best terms you're willing to offer or something less, perhaps much less. After all, if you bid less, the seller might just accept it or at least be anchored by it, so that even if the price rises during a negotiation,

TABLE 14-3

Zeswitz Music, acquisition financial model, version 3, with reduced capital expenditures

KEY ASSUMPTIONS	
Purchase price as a multiple of 2012 EBITDA ($1,535)*	4
Leverage ratio, bank	30%
Debt rate, bank	6%
Leverage ratio, seller	30%
Debt rate, seller	8%

HYPOTHETICAL ACQUISITION FUNDING

Uses		Sources	
Purchase price	6,140	Bank debt	1,887
Acquisition costs	150	Seller debt	1,887
		Investor equity	2,516
	6,290		6,290

YEAR ENDING DECEMBER 31

	2013	2014	2015	2016	2017
Free cash flow from table 13-3	763	801	841	883	928
50% of capital expenditures	272	286	300	315	331
	1,035	1,087	1,141	1,198	1,259
Exit (4 x the 2017 EBITDA of $1,590 from table 13-3)					6,360
Bank debt					
Beginning debt	1,887	1,116	247	0	0
Interest on debt	113	67	15	0	0
Debt repayment	771	869	247	0	0
Ending debt	1,116	227	0	0	0
Seller debt					
Beginning debt	1,887	1,887	1,887	1,159	54
Interest on debt	151	151	151	93	4
Debt repayment	0	0	728	1,105	54
Ending debt	1,887	1,887	1,159	54	0
Available equity cash flow after debt payments	0	0	0	0	7,560
IRR to owner plus equity investors**	25%				

Note: Unless marked as a percentage or a multiple for the purchase price, all numbers are in thousands of dollars.

*EBITDA, earnings before interest, taxes, depreciation, and amortization.

**IRR, internal rate of return.

you will still be well below the highest price and the best terms you are willing to offer. Alternatively, you could bid the highest price and best terms you are willing to offer, recognizing that you are not committed to the acquisition at that price and that you can negotiate it down if you discover something you don't like about the prospect during confirmatory due diligence. Finally, there is an even more extreme approach: Bid *more* than you are willing to pay to lock in the LOI—get the seller to sign off on the basic terms of the acquisition—and then plan on a downward renegotiation.

While theories on price negotiation vary, we suggest leaving a bit of room to adjust pricing and terms as the deal evolves. Don't bid your highest possible price at the start; just offer a fair price and terms.

Creating an Indication of Interest (IOI)

After you have completed much of your preliminary due diligence and acquisition model, you should consider sending the seller an indication of interest (IOI). The IOI usually is just a short letter that contains your offer price and a few other details about the proposed transaction. It isn't binding on either the buyer or the seller; sometimes it is even less formal and takes place orally through a conversation with the broker, who then communicates the information to the seller. The purpose of the IOI is just to get an agreement on pricing, even if it is just a range, before you invest time on the other terms and conditions of the offer.

In Randy's consideration of Zeswitz, for example, his modeling suggested that he would acquire the business for 4x EBITDA. Consequently, before he invested more time in the prospect, it made sense for him to send an IOI with an offer price of $6.14 million or less. Appendix A contains the IOI Randy sent to Zeswitz's broker (we'll discuss the other terms in chapter 15).

Even if the seller is unwilling to accept your price, the IOI provides an opportunity for the seller to reply with additional information, such as more recent financial results or an additional explanation for an add-back. The more meaningful the response you get, the more seriously your offer is likely being treated by the seller. That response might lead you to update your offer price, and if so, you'll work to negotiate a price that is acceptable to you and the seller.

Next Steps

Pricing is the most important part of an offer but not the only part. The next chapter discusses the other acquisition terms that will be part of your preliminary offer.

NOTE

1. Gemini Investors V, LP, Confidential Offering Memorandum.

CHAPTER 15

Deal Terms

The seller isn't just interested in the price you'll pay for their company. They also want to know where you will get the money, when you will pay, what (exactly) you are buying, how long the process will take, and their time commitment to the business after the sale. Answers to these questions help the seller assess your ability to close the deal, your offer price, and the postsale plans—important aspects of the deal for any seller to evaluate. Before you can make the offer, you need to determine your position on each of these important parameters.

How You Are Financing the Acquisition

If you are like most buyers, you will use a combination of debt and equity to finance your purchase. We will discuss both of these in more detail later, as you get closer to the actual acquisition. At this point, you will need to discover approximately what percent of the purchase price lenders will be willing to lend, how much investors will be willing to invest, and how much seller debt the seller can be expected to hold.

Debt

Debt, a fixed claim of the firm, requires the firm to make prespecified interest and principal payments or face significant adverse consequences. The debt will come in the form of a loan from a bank, nonbank lenders, and sellers.

Most buyers use *senior loans*—that is, loans that stand first in line to be paid—to cover between one-third and one-half of the cost of their acquisition. Senior loans—often from a bank—have the highest-priority claim on the cash flows and assets of the business. As you are researching a financing plan, contact a handful of local banks and discuss whether your potential acquisition would qualify for a bank loan, particularly one backed by the Small Business Administration (SBA) if you are acquiring a company in the United States. Ask how big such a loan might be and at what rate. If the answer is yes, you'd qualify, that's great; the loan amount you are given should form the core of your financing plan. If not, you will need to rely more on other sources, such as nonbank lenders and seller financing.

Approximately 1,500 of the 7,500 banks in the United States participate in the SBA's flagship small-business financing program to provide loans for these kinds of acquisitions. If you qualify, this excellent vehicle for obtaining a loan for your acquisition enjoys four advantages over typical bank debt. First, you can borrow more money than you can with other kinds of loans: The SBA will allow you to borrow up to 80% of the acquisition cost of qualifying small businesses up to a maximum loan size of $5.0 million (conventional lenders typically lend 40% to 50% of the acquisition cost). Second, because three-quarters of the loan is guaranteed by the SBA, it is less expensive than other bank debt. Third, the loan is long term, typically ten years. And fourth, as long as you meet your required payments, there are few other requirements to meet during the life of the loan.

If your acquisition doesn't qualify for a bank loan, you can still borrow from nonbank lenders such as finance companies or private lending partnerships. These lenders are often willing to lend when banks are not and are willing to customize loans in ways that banks are unable to do. On the other hand, nonbank lenders often require extensive covenants that are typically more stringent than bank covenants. The cost of nonbank debt is typically much higher than the cost of bank debt.

All of these loans are senior loans and must be paid first, ahead of other creditors and equity holders (other than tax distributions made to equity holders to pay income taxes). If you don't make scheduled payments, the senior loan holder also has first claim on your company's assets, which can be sold to repay the loan. Senior bank loans often require collateral and a personal guarantee and will require the business to meet certain operational and financial metrics during the life of the loan.

Seller debt

Most buyers finance about one-third of the cost of their acquisition directly from the seller. Beyond providing financing, *seller debt* creates an economic incentive for the seller to help the business succeed after its sale. Seller notes are an obligation from the company to the seller and generally have interest rates that are slightly higher than bank loans. They are subordinate to any senior loans, so if the company defaults, the senior loan gets fully paid before the seller note collects anything. Seller notes generally do not receive personal guarantees or have covenants with financial tests. However, it is common for seller notes to have restrictions on adding additional senior debt or on distributing cash to equity holders while the seller note remains outstanding.

Earn-outs are similar to seller notes in that in these arrangements, part of the sales price is paid on a deferred basis. But in the case of earn-outs, that payment is pegged to company performance. It enables the seller to be paid a higher price if future company performance hits certain targets, while the buyer has the protection of only paying more if the company demonstrates this additional success.

An earn-out is a good way to resolve different views of company value during a purchase negotiation. For example, when Greg Mazur was negotiating to buy Great Eastern Premium Pet Foods (GEPP), an earn-out arrangement helped him close a disagreement about valuation. Over the prior two years, GEPP's revenues had increased by about 15%. The seller projected strong continuing growth and initially sought a price of $2.5 million. Greg liked the business but knew that the pet food market was mature. He thought this mature market would ultimately limit how fast GEPP could grow. He negotiated a deal to pay $1.24 million at closing (about 4x EBITDA), with an earn-out of 1% of annual sales in each of the following five years. The seller believed that these terms brought him closer to his pricing goal and Mazur knew that the earn-out would be significant only if GEPP was successful under his future ownership—not to mention that the earn-out would align the interests of the seller with Mazur's in the five years following the transition.

Equity

You will also need to raise funds from investors who are typically family, friends, and high-net-worth individuals in your network; the amount of the purchase price that isn't financed with debt or seller financing will come from equity. Equity has no prespecified payments, and equity investors share in the risk of the business with the entrepreneur—that's you. Generally, equity investors in small firms require that their capital be repaid before you get any significant payments, and then you and the equity investors share in the benefits of ownership.

If you followed our advice from chapter 5, "Paying for Your Search," you have kept in contact with potential investors throughout your search, whether they are funders of your search, advisors, or simply individuals whom you identified as potential future investors. You should now approach them to gauge their interest in providing equity to finance your acquisition. They will want to hear about the business of the prospect, its historical performance, the terms of your purchase, the likely rates of return, and other metrics such as the amount, type, and cost of debt you will use. Before you make your offer, you need to be sure that there is sufficient interest from potential equity investors at the specific price and financing plan you are considering.

Transaction Structure

The actual acquisition of the company can take two forms: buying the company's *stock* or its *assets*. Generally, buying assets is more favorable to you as a buyer because you obtain the operating business while leaving behind all liabilities other than those you specifically agreed to assume. An asset purchase minimizes the chances of a nasty surprise from finding undisclosed liabilities after your purchase. There are also substantial tax advantages available to buyers who purchase assets. Occasionally, however, it is only practical to buy stock: With C-corporations in the United States, for example, there are prohibitive taxes involved with asset purchases, and sometimes there are licenses or third-party contracts that are difficult to transfer from the seller to the buyer, except by selling the stock of the company. If your prospect is a C-corporation, we strongly suggest getting professional tax advice early on, certainly when you are considering the offer price and when you are deciding on the specific terms of the proposed transaction.

You'll also want to explicitly make your offer on a debt-free, cash-free basis, as explained in chapter 12, "Filtering for the Owner's Commitment to Sell." Such a basis means that the seller is responsible for paying off any loans owed by the business before the acquisition and that he or she gets to keep any cash on hand.

Working Capital Peg

Most assets—the building, the equipment, the trucks, the customer lists, and so forth—don't change dramatically between your offer and the completion of the acquisition. However, working capital—receivables, inventory, accounts payable, and accrued expenses—changes every day. Your deal will need to specify both how much net working capital will be left in the company at closing— the *working capital peg*—and what the adjustment to the purchase price will be if the working capital amount on the closing date turns out to be different from the promised amount. Generally, the peg is set so that when you close on your acquisition, you should have neither a net working capital deficiency, which forces you to invest more money into the business, nor an excess, which allows you to draw out a cash distribution.

Timing of Closing and Exclusivity

Most sellers end up being surprised at how much time elapses between their agreeing to an acquisition and the closing: It is at least three or four months. During that time, you will invest much time and money into confirmatory due diligence, raising debt and equity financing, and structuring the legal documents associated with the acquisition. We cover those tasks in part V, "Completing the Acquisition." You want to know that the seller is working in good faith with you and only you. Buyers will often propose a closing date and exclusivity period that seems reasonable—say, 90 days—but this time is likely to be extended.

Transition Period

You will probably want the seller to help with the transition of the business over to you after the sale. The seller can introduce you to key customers and suppliers, can help teach you how the firm operates on a day-to-day basis, and can provide you with management advice. The length of this transition period depends on the complexity of the company, your familiarity with the business and its industry, and your relationship with the seller. Three months of full-time commitment from the seller is generally sensible, with occasional access thereafter for up to a year. A longer period can stall the organization after the transaction, and a shorter arrangement may not give sufficient time for your education. You will also want to agree on a noncompete period for the seller. In such an agreement, the seller cannot take on a role that is in competition with the original business. Generally, noncompete agreements with sellers are four or five years long.

Next Steps

With the offer price and deal terms in hand, you are ready to structure the acquisition offer. That's the topic of the next chapter.

CHAPTER 16

The Offer

With your decisions about the price you are willing to pay for the prospect and the key terms of your proposed deal, you are ready to make an offer. This is a big step. If your offer is accepted, you will spend much of the next several months completing the transaction and then, perhaps, a significant period of your life managing the business.

The offer itself takes the form of a formal letter of intent (LOI). In this document, you'll state your proposed deal terms, including an initial offer price and the specifics of the next phase of the acquisition. Ideally, the seller will accept your LOI by formally signing it, but more often, some negotiation has to happen first.

Letter of Intent (LOI)

Your LOI is a detailed agreement that describes your deal. First, it specifies in writing the key terms of the deal: the purchase price, the amount and terms of seller debt, any business assets not included in the sale, the amount of working capital delivered at the closing, the length of a postsale noncompete from the owner, and any other material deal points. If you go forward with the acquisition, the LOI will be succeeded by a much more detailed and binding purchase agreement. But the LOI insures that there is mutual understanding of the key terms before everyone does a lot more work. While the LOI doesn't commit either you or the seller to complete the proposed acquisition at its price and terms, it anchors both of you. Of course, the deal might change as a result of any new information that comes up in due diligence, but the LOI is a handshake and it allows both parties to proceed with reasonable confidence.

The only terms that are legally binding in the LOI are those that have to do with the structure of the closing: the exclusivity of your offer and your own promises regarding confidentiality of the information and nonsolicitation of the seller's customers and employees. The exclusivity is important to you because you are about to invest a lot of time into confirmatory due diligence and raising debt and equity financing—you want to know that the seller is working in good faith with you and only you. The confidentiality and nonsolicitation are important to the seller in case your proposed deal doesn't close.

If you have already submitted an IOI on this prospect, there will be much overlap between the IOI and the LOI. The LOI is likely to have more details because the back and forth during the IOI process helped define the seller's concerns and your responses. Also, you'll now know more about the prospect and the likely financing opportunities.

Items to include

Your LOI should specify the key terms of the deal that you've worked out over the past few chapters, including the following:

- Offer price

- Transaction structure (purchase of stock or assets)

- Amount and terms of seller debt

- Amount of working capital delivered at the closing (the working capital peg)

- Timing of closing and exclusivity period

- Transition period and length of a postsale non-compete from the owner

- Your confidentiality and nonsolicitation agreement

You can see what an LOI looks like in appendix B, a hypothetical LOI for Randy's acquisition of Zeswitz. While the letter closely resembles Randy's actual LOI, we've changed some of the details to protect Randy and the seller. So while you can use the sample LOI as a starting point, you'll probably need to customize it for issues unique to your deal or things that your seller is particularly focused on. And if you're not comfortable with your own reading of the LOI and its terms, you should have your attorney review it before sending it to the seller.

How much detail is enough

You'll need to decide how much detail should be included in your LOI. The primary advantage of a detailed LOI is that material issues are identified and negotiated before a lot of time and expense is spent. The primary disadvantages are that the seller may not be ready to negotiate through a set of difficult issues early on. Remember: It is likely that the seller is selling a company for the first time and doesn't have a good grasp of all the steps to complete a transaction. Forcing the seller into early, uncomfortable discussions may damage your relationship with the seller and make a deal harder to complete.

Perhaps the thorniest LOI term is the working capital peg, because the appropriate amount of detail is uncertain. As explained in chapter 15, this peg specifies the amount of working capital that will be left in the business. Sellers seem to understand the concept of a cash-free, debt-free deal yet balk at leaving a set amount of working capital in the business. Often, the seller simply doesn't have the detailed monthly financial statements that would be used to estimate the working capital on the closing date. Consequently, you, the buyer, will have difficulty proposing a specific amount, and the seller will be hesitant to accept it. None of the choices are perfect:

1. You could insist on resolving the dollar amount of the working capital peg in the LOI. That will delay the LOI, perhaps by several weeks, as the seller collects the historical financial informa-

tion. During that time, you will either delay the next steps in the deal—risking frustration by the seller—or will invest heavily in the deal without an exclusivity agreement.

2. You could ignore the working capital issue in the LOI and negotiate it when you negotiate the purchase agreement. The advantage is that the financial information will be available; the disadvantage is that the seller may treat this as renegotiating the deal and terminate discussions.

3. You could specify that the deal will include a working capital peg and describe its calculation but do not assign a specific dollar amount. For example, you could agree that the peg will be equal to the average net working capital over the six months prior to the LOI.

We have seen searchers pursue all three of these paths. We like the first choice the least because our experience is that sellers are not ready for the discussion, and good deals are too likely be abandoned over the issue. We don't like the second path much, either. We have seen deals be delayed for months—and the relationship between the buyer and the seller severely damaged—by delaying the discussion of the working capital peg until the purchase agreement negotiations. For these reasons, we recommend the third choice—defining the issue and establishing the formula—as a reasonable balance between the desire to resolve issues in the LOI and the expediency of delaying them.

The working capital peg is, of course, only one of many issues that you'll need to settle by the time you complete the transaction. Thus, the balance between resolving issues and delaying them is a judgment call throughout much of the LOI. It is likely that you will need to let some of these issues remain vague while others will be resolved early. Terms that are easily defined should be defined—for example, the interest rate, maturity date, and principal repayment schedule on the proposed seller note. Keep in mind that an LOI typically runs 4 pages long; your binding purchase agreement is about 40 pages. You want to agree only on key deal points in the LOI; greater detail is reserved for the purchase agreement.

Getting the Seller to Sign

As you weigh whether to resolve issues up front or to delay negotiations until later, be careful not to compromise on terms in the LOI. You don't want to make it so easy for the seller to sign that you struggle to get the acquisition completed down the road—your ultimate goal. You shouldn't enter into an LOI if you are unwilling to complete the acquisition on the terms you describe.

The LOI is your offer, and though you are hoping that the seller will accept, at least four responses are possible. First, and most disappointing, is no response at all. Second, the seller might reply with a higher price and different terms. Third, the seller might use the offer as an opportunity to provide you with more information about the company in hopes of raising your perception of the value of the company. And fourth, the seller may accept the offer with only a few, minor revisions and return to you a countersigned LOI. With the first response, you're out of luck; with the fourth, you're *very* lucky. With the second and third responses, you will consider any new information or renegotiate in response to their counter-offer until either both of you sign an amended LOI or it becomes clear you can't agree and you move on.

Next Steps

If the seller doesn't sign the LOI, you'll need to try to negotiate a deal that works for both of you. Sometimes, the seller really cares about a particular provision of the LOI, and because the provision is less meaningful to you, a revised deal is easy to craft. Other times, a renegotiated deal is much tougher but still possible. And, of course, many times, there is no common ground and you'll need to move on to another prospect. If that happens, be sure to check back with the seller periodically; sellers often find deals more appealing after they've gone several months without a better offer or after a seemingly better deal with another buyer fell apart.

If the seller signs the LOI, the next steps are bringing the proposed transaction to a successful completion. You need to complete confirmatory due diligence, arrange debt and equity financing, and structure the detailed description of the acquisition in the binding asset pur-chase agreement. All of these steps are covered in part V, "Completing the Acquisition."

PART FIVE

Completing the Acquisition

You now have a signed LOI for a business that meets your qualifications; your offer has been accepted. Now begins the most intensive part of the process: completing the acquisition. Part V walks you through the steps of confirming your preliminary due diligence, raising capital for your purchase, negotiating the purchase agreement, and, finally, getting to closing day—and beyond.

We begin in **chapter 17, "Confirmatory Due Diligence,"** when you gain inside access to the prospect to learn more about it. Hopefully, this due diligence will reconfirm why you like the company and will uncover nothing that causes you to abandon the acquisition. While confirmatory due diligence is mainly your effort, you will begin to spend significant amounts of money on outside professionals for the first time since you began the search process. You also need to secure financing, and we discuss this issue in **chapter 18, "Raising Debt,"** and **chapter 19, "Raising Acquisition Equity."** The purchase agreement defines the specific terms of your acquisition and is full of important details that you and your lawyer will negotiate with the seller and the seller's lawyer; we discuss the important provisions in **chapter 20, "Negotiating the Purchase Agreement."** Finally, we end part V with some thoughts about the closing day and the first few weeks of running your company in **chapter 21, "The Closing Day and Beyond."**

CHAPTER 17

Confirmatory Due Diligence

Until now, your research and preliminary due diligence allowed you to explore and analyze the prospect's business model. You accepted the seller's answers to your questions with little supporting evidence. During confirmatory due diligence, you will validate your understanding of the essential elements of the business with a cross-check of the company's documentation and with the advice of experts such as accountants and attorneys. This is also your chance to explore other aspects of the business to be sure there are no undiscovered negatives that could affect your willingness to acquire the business.

Overview

The process begins when the LOI is signed. If your LOI specifies an exclusivity period of 90 days, you'll want to complete the bulk of your confirmatory due diligence in the first 30 days so that you have time for negotiating the purchase agreement and finalizing your arrangements to raise debt and equity. For the first week or two, you should conduct confirmatory diligence on your own. You'll meet with the owner, learn about the records the company has readily available, go over the financials with the chief financial officer (CFO), and then complete a *proof of cash*, an analysis that confirms the revenues and expenses reported in the financial statements by comparing them to deposits and payments to and from the company's bank account.

Your next step is to involve your accountant, your lawyer, and possibly other specialists (see the sidebar "Selecting Professional Advisors" for advice on finding the best experts for your situation). But you should always sequence due-diligence tasks so that the big issues, if any, are identified early, before you hire your advisors and waste time and money on a deal that can't go forward.

SELECTING PROFESSIONAL ADVISORS

Your two most important advisors during your confirmatory due diligence will be your **accountant** and your **lawyer**. Find professionals who are specifically experienced in the purchase and sale of smaller firms. An experienced accountant will have a good sense of the common risks in smaller firms' accounting practices and will focus on areas like payroll tax, sales tax, and proper accounting for noncash expenses like bad debt reserves or accruals for sales force bonuses that are

SELECTING PROFESSIONAL ADVISORS

earned but not yet paid. These items are best examined by your accountant, who will have established procedures to quickly determine if the company has accurately recorded these expenses. Similarly, an experienced lawyer will know which contracts to focus on and typical terms and conditions. Again, you need to conduct this due diligence economically, so hiring experienced professionals who know where to focus is important.

You should expect that accounting due diligence will cost $20,000 to $50,000. Where you will fall in this wide range depends on how much work needs to be done to understand the company's true financial performance. Legal due diligence is more tightly scoped and includes the cost of preparing the purchase agreement and related documents; fees for these tasks usually cost about $75,000. Other specialty advisors you may require include engineering consultants to examine machinery and equipment, a software consultant to review software upgrade needs, or an environmental consultant to review usage history on industrial real estate. The cost of specialty advisors, if they are needed at all, is typically much more modest.

While your professional advisors will provide valuable analysis and advice, you cannot fully delegate anything: There are no such things as accounting issues or legal issues that you completely turn over to others. You should be at the very center of all due-diligence activities because they tie so closely to the deal you will ultimately strike and to how you will operate the business. To decide if your advisors have confirmed particular facts to your satisfaction and can move on to the next task or if new questions are raised by their findings, you should have regular discussions with your advisors—perhaps every day—as they complete pieces of work. Like so many parts of becoming an entrepreneur through acquisition, it is an iterative process that you guide.

As you proceed, there are six fundamental areas you need to assess to make sure you are actually buying what you think you are buying:

- ☐ The character—and specifically the honesty—of the seller

- ☐ The company's accounts and finances (accounting due diligence)

- ☐ The company's contracts and legal affairs (legal due diligence)

- ☐ Customer perspectives

- ☐ Employee perspectives

- ☐ Any further specialized due diligence

Honesty and Character

Character assessment is the most basic of the due-diligence building blocks: Before you go any further, evaluate whether the owner of the business you are buying is truthful. If you feel that the seller is not an honest person, move on to another deal. No matter how thor-

ough your due diligence, sellers always have an information advantage over buyers; your odds of outsmarting a
dishonest owner are low.

You have had several conversations with the seller
since you first identified the prospect, and you probably
met face-to-face during your preliminary due diligence.
You should have a good gut sense of the seller's character, but confirmatory due diligence gives you new information to update your evaluation in three ways:

- Throughout the due-diligence process, you will see
  whether your independent verification of facts about
  the business unearths negative issues that the seller
  didn't volunteer frankly. If you present the owner
  with a negative fact discovered in due diligence,
  how does he or she explain not having previously
  reported it to you? Truthfulness is a habit—if a seller
  has covered up one thing, it is likely that the seller
  has covered up other things that you haven't found.

- When you interview customers, ask them how they
  view the firm's or the owner's integrity. Have disputes or misunderstandings been resolved fairly?
  Does the company deliver what it promised, or
  more, but never less?

- When you examine the company's business
  practices—billing; customer refunds; quality
  control; and employee pay, benefits, and evalu-
  ations—are all parties being treated fairly? How
  owners treat their customers and workers is a good
  indication of how they will treat you.

Accounting Due Diligence

The work of accounting due diligence is shared between you and a hired accountant. Start by taking a first pass through the material from a business perspective. This first pass can reveal deal killers; finding them early means you won't have paid accounting fees on a deal that will never close. In addition, your familiarity with the company's financial information will enable you to guide your accountant's work. Then the accountant can focus on a more detailed review of the financials—particularly any area in which you felt something might be awry.

There are two separate streams of accounting due diligence. In a *proof of cash,* you verify the accuracy of the company's historical accounting reports. With a *quality of earnings analysis,* you assess the makeup of the company's historical revenues and earnings to determine whether they are representative of future performance and likely to recur.

First pass of financial statements

In your first pass through the company's financial statements on your own, look for any significant inconsistencies or inaccuracies in historical revenue and EBITDA. These can be common; most small firms do not have audited financial reports or robust internal financial reporting systems. And while simplified accounting may be adequate for the entrepreneur to operate a business, the reporting errors that accompany such a system don't work for a buyer, because they can result in misleading historical results that affect your purchase price.

A common problem, for example, is timing errors in revenues and associated costs: If costs are recognized in the first year of a project and revenue is recognized in the second year, the company will seem much more profitable in the second year. If the second year happens to be the year of sale and you based your purchase price on the reported EBITDA from that year, this timing error may make your acquisition price too high. Because the company is small, the scope of misreporting doesn't need to be very large to have a material effect on profits and purchase price. As you initially familiarize yourself with the company's accounts, ask about the causes of large year-to-year fluctuations in revenue, expenses, and EBITDA; these can be the result of inaccurate accounting records.

Proof of cash

Checking accounting statements for accuracy also calls for comparing different forms of documentation. One important confirmatory comparison of documents is a proof-of-cash analysis. Imagine, for example, that your acquisition candidate's financial reports show that, in each of the last three years, sales were $10.0 million and EBITDA was $2.0 million and that, of the $2.0 EBITDA, $0.5 million was used for capital expenditures and $1.5 million was distributed to the owner.

You can perform a simple first-pass test on the accuracy of these reports by taking the company's monthly bank statements and adding up all the deposits and all the payments. The deposits ought to roughly equal the $10.0 million made in sales; the payments ought to roughly equal the $10.0 million of the year's revenue that has been spent or distributed to the owner. Identify and add back the owner's distributions, and the remaining payments should come pretty close to $8.5 million. You have just confirmed that the company's financial reports showing $10.0 million of revenue, $8.5 million of expenditures, and $1.5 million of cash flow is supported by $10.0 million of bank deposits and $8.5 million of checks written to third parties.

This won't be a precise analysis: Accounts receivable and accounts payable will be growing and shrinking, and inventory might have changed—but the numbers shouldn't be far off. If you perform this test on the previous three years of bank statements and the EBITDA-less-capital-expenditure number you keep coming to is closer to zero than $1.5 million, then you approach the seller for an explanation before you bring in your outside accountant.

There are different ways to validate your target's financial statements. Greg Geronemus and David Rosner's commonsense approach was based on the idea that no one reports a *higher* income to the IRS than they actually earn. As the two men did their due diligence on SmarTours, a group travel service to exotic locations, they compared pretax income reported in the company's financial statements to the pretax income reported in the company's federal income tax returns. They had some reconciling to do since income tax calculations are different from income statement calculations. But the match between income from the tax return and income from the financial statements was a pretty good first-pass test on the accuracy of those statements.

As you review the financials, keep an eye out for various discrepancies:

- ☐ Timing between the reporting of revenues and associated costs (resulting in inaccurate EBITDA during the period on which the sale price is based)

- ☐ Actual cash flow as shown in bank statements versus reported figures for revenue, expenditures, and owner distributions

- ☐ Pretax income as reported in financial statements versus that in tax returns

- ☐ Big fluctuations in year-to-year revenues, expenses, and EBITDA

Once you have done a first pass on the basic accuracy of the financials, it is time to bring in your accountant to review the financials more thoroughly. You should also ask your accountant to report on the competence of the company's accounting department. Is the CFO adequate for the job? Is there proper separation of duties to avoid fraud or stealing by employees? Finally, your accountant should also provide a quality-of-earnings report and an assessment of any tax risks, which we'll discuss next.

Quality-of-earnings review

Even correctly prepared statements do not tell you everything you need to know. This is because you're interested in whether historical revenue and profit will recur in the future, while accounting statements only reflect the past. That is where the quality-of-earnings analysis comes in.

The *quality-of-earnings analysis* is a quantitatively based assessment that uses historical financial results to estimate the *future* performance of the business. As part of your preliminary due diligence, you studied the historical financials and EBITDA to understand how they have fluctuated. Now is the time to examine any fluctuations more fully because you now have access to detailed financial records that should allow you to confirm your understanding.

Your accountant should take the lead in this work, but you'll be fully involved. Start by taking the last several years of financials, and ask the company's CFO to show you the components of each line item. Break out revenue by major customer and by product. Do sales concentrate with a few clients? If so, check the patterns of their purchasing in each of the last few years. Are the major clients steady and recurring, or do they come and go? Were there any large pieces of business that only happened once? Did the business get a new customer? Did it expand operations?

Don't just look at revenues: Examine the individual cost categories that make up each expense line item. Is there a reason to think that any big cost is likely to go up? If payroll is a big component of total expenses, it's a good idea to check that employees are currently being paid a market rate and not below. If rent expense is a big item, check the remaining term of the lease and whether the rate is likely to change substantially at renewal. Did the company reduce costs by delaying annual maintenance on machinery? The purpose of this work is to prove to yourself that the historical revenues and expenses, and therefore the historical pretax profit performance you are buying, is likely to recur.

Also look at add-backs. If you accepted the seller's representations about the add-backs when you decided on your offer price for the prospect, you should reexamine those carefully now. You will need to look at the records and decide whether these are truly appropriate to be added back. You will need to gauge whether certain expenses are really personal or whether a onetime expense is truly not going to recur under your ownership. It's typical to negotiate over the type and amount of included add-backs.

Tax risks

Most smaller firms are organized as *flow-through entities* for income tax purposes, meaning that their income tax liability flows through the company and is an obligation of the business's shareholders rather than of the company itself. This means you don't have to check that the company correctly calculated and paid prior year income taxes; if there is an income tax audit and additional taxes are owed, the obligation flows through to whoever was the owner in that year, and it is their responsibility to address any errors. Sometimes the company you are buying was established as a C-corporation (the type of structure in the United States; similar structures exist in other countries), and the company itself is the taxpayer and not its shareholders. Your accountant will then need to carefully examine prior annual income tax returns for accurate reporting because if the tax authorities audit a prior year and assess more tax, the company owes that back tax even though you, the new share owner, didn't own the company at that time.

There are other types of tax underpayments that stay with the company you purchase even if it is a flow-through entity. The largest of these payments are payroll taxes and sales taxes. Suppose your target uses 45 independent contractors to sell its products, paying them a fee each time one of them makes a sale. Because the salespeople are independent contractors and not employees, the company pays no Social Security tax, no federal or state payroll tax, and no unemployment insurance taxes. But do these salespeople meet the guidelines for independent contractors, or are they actually employees? The rules are complex and subject to some amount of judgment. But if these contractors are later deemed to be employees, the company will face a significant increase in payroll tax expense. Even worse, there could be a liability to the company for prior years' payroll taxes that should have been paid but weren't.

Here is another potential problem: Imagine that the company you are buying provides services across 30 states and numerous municipalities. Does it collect sales and use tax as prescribed in each of these many jurisdictions? Many smaller firms are simply unaware of their sales and use tax obligations in other jurisdictions. You had nothing to do with the company's past practice, but if you buy the company, you could find yourself assessed for sales taxes that should have been collected over the years—as far back as the founding of the company.

This tax analysis will all be done by your accountant without much involvement by you, as it requires specialized training and experience. Meanwhile, you can focus on other confirmatory diligence.

Legal Due Diligence

Almost every business has contracts that are important to its operation—a lease on its headquarters, a distribution agreement on its largest-selling product, or employment and noncompete agreements with several key salespeople. You need to read all of the company's important contracts and make sure they are consistent with your plans for the business. You'll need to understand which contracts require consent from the other party to transfer the contract to you, and what kind of performance or payment guarantees have been made. Most commercial contracts are straightforward and easy to understand. But if a particular contract is critical to the business, or if you read one but don't understand it, have your lawyer review those as well.

How can you be sure that the seller is presenting you with all of the company's contractual commitments? The purchase agreement your attorney will prepare requires the seller to list every such contract on an attached schedule. This enables you to identify and review each contractual obligation of the company before you sign the purchase agreement. If you review the schedule and it lists a contract you haven't read, simply ask for it.

Contracts such as leases or distribution agreements often have *change-of-control consents,* which mean that if the firm or its assets are sold, consent is required from the other party to transfer the contract to the company's new owner. If the business relationships with the partners as they currently stand are satisfactory, this is usually straightforward; you should just budget time for you or the seller to collect any required consents.

Building leases to smaller firms often are personally guaranteed by the seller; when you buy the company, the seller (quite reasonably) will want to be removed from the guarantee. You will need to persuade the property owner that the creditworthiness of your purchasing entity is at least as good as that of the seller. In addition, the proprietors will sometimes seek a fee or an improvement in lease terms in return for their consent.

Customer Interviews

As part of your confirmatory due-diligence investigation, you will take on a particularly delicate part of the process: interviews with customers of the target company. This can be difficult to arrange with the seller, since most owners don't want to announce a sale until they feel confident that it is actually going to occur to avoid rumors spreading. At the same time, you absolutely must speak to customers to learn the strengths and weaknesses of the company, to confirm current industry trends, and to validate your business plan for the company.

Generally, owners permit customer interviews toward the end of the diligence period—when confidence is high that the transaction will proceed. The buyer and seller agree on a sample of customers who will be interviewed, and the seller introduces the buyer to them. Five or six good quality interviews should be enough to confirm what you have been told about customer behavior and satisfaction. Here are questions you want to ask:

- What qualities do customers look for in selecting their supplier?

- Are they satisfied with the services of the company? How is the company better or worse than the competition?

- What causes the customers to switch suppliers?

- Do they anticipate changes in the amount of business they will be doing with the company?

If you were unclear after reading the confidential information memorandum and interviewing the owner about how customers select a supplier and what keeps them from switching, you may want to move customer interviews earlier in your due diligence process. One way to get around the seller's understandable caution in the earlier stages of the deal is to reach out not to the company's customers but to similar consumers in a different geographical area. Early in his diligence on Zeswitz Music, for example, Randy Shayler interviewed school band directors *outside* the company's service area. You will quickly learn about how customers in this business select a supplier, how they rank their current suppliers, and how frequently they switch—and you can apply all this knowledge to your target company.

Employee Interviews

You will also need to interview the company's employees. In a smaller firm, this group is likely to contain only a handful of people: a couple of managers, the CFO, and any key salespeople. It is likely the seller has told the key employees about the pending sale at this point, if only because these employees have information the seller needs to support the confirmatory due-diligence process. Still, sellers will probably be hesitant to allow these interviews, which commonly occur late in confirmatory due diligence.

Employees will naturally be cautious in responding to your questions; it is unrealistic to expect negative revelations about the company. Your goal for these interviews is rather to assess the capabilities of your critical employees. Think of yourself as conducting job interviews: Are these the people you have confidence in? Do they understand the role of their job in the larger mission of the company, or are they robotic order takers? Do they demonstrate energy and commitment to excellence, or are they impatiently waiting for quitting time to roll around? Are they experienced and knowledgeable about the business?

Your customer interviews will have given you insights about what matters to clients. Find out if the company's managers and salespeople are closely tuned into what their customers value or are detached from their own market.

Employee interviews give you an opportunity to learn how the company gets its job done. Try this seemingly simple question to begin each interview: "So, what do you do here?" You will learn how a customer order turns into a completed, delivered product or service. Here are a few other questions that will help you discover the capability of the company's managers:

- What do the company's customers care about most with regard to the service you provide?

- How well do you think you measure up to their expectations?

- Do you think there is anything the company could be doing better?

Specialized Due Diligence

The first five building blocks of due diligence (character, accounting, legal, customers, and employees) apply to any company that you consider buying. Sometimes, however, you'll need to hire an expert to examine a specific business asset, liability, or risk. Most commonly, this specialized need will fall into one of four areas:

- **Machinery and equipment** may be key assets of the business, but you probably do not have the expertise to assess their remaining useful life, the needed upgrades or repairs, and whether any equipment is obsolete from a competitive perspective. Hire engineering consultants to evaluate plant equipment and answer these questions.

- **Software systems** may be central to the company's operation. Retain a software consultant to review software documentation, security, the need for upgrade investments, and other factors that affect system reliability or the requirements for additional investment.

- **Environmental hazards** are a potential risk if the company cannot practically move from its facility and particularly if it owns the underlying real estate. Have an environmental consultant check the usage history of a property. If there were prior industrial activities using hazardous chemicals, the consultant will perform soil tests to ensure that no environmental liability attaches to the company. Note that lenders may also require that this work be done and presented to them in advance of providing a loan.

- **Regulatory compliance and rules changes** are critical in certain businesses such as health care, waste disposal, broadcasting, and many others. If the company operates in a highly regulated field, arrange for a compliance review by a lawyer specialized in this area (different from your acquisition attorney). This expert will confirm that the company has all the required permits and is operating in compliance with rules, and he or she will advise you on any regulatory changes that might affect the business.

What to Do with What You Learn

You may be able to tell quickly from your confirmatory due diligence that the owner painted too rosy a picture in your initial conversations, but this doesn't need to spell the end of the deal. Randy Shayler's acquisition of Zeswitz Music is a prime example: During confirmatory due diligence, Randy discovered that the size of the company's instrument inventory was 15% smaller than reported and that current-year EBITDA was 20% lower. Zeswitz's owner hadn't been trying to mislead; as with many smaller firms, the company's financial reporting systems were basic and its accounting staff was spread thin. Rather than giving up, Randy negotiated the purchase price to reflect the lower, more accurate performance numbers and successfully purchased the company in the summer of 2013.

At the conclusion of your confirmatory due diligence, you will take one of four actions:

- **Close the deal as agreed.** The due diligence confirms what you have been told and what you believe about the company.

- **Adjust the price.** The financial performance was different from how it was represented, but the differences are small enough that the buyer and seller can compromise through a price reduction, a shift of dollars from fixed purchase price to earn-out, or other means.

- **Change contract terms.** You change the contract terms when you discover a specific liability or risk. Typical ways of addressing an identified risk include having the seller indemnify the buyer for that risk, requiring that a larger amount from the purchase price be held in escrow, or restructuring the deal to acquire assets instead of company stock so that the seller retains certain liabilities instead of passing them on you.

- **Walk away.** The historical financial performance is significantly worse than represented; the company's future prospects look poor; big investments are needed; or other materially adverse factors are discovered—in other words, whenever the company's condition is dramatically different from what you had previously understood.

A last word of advice: Throughout the process, don't become bogged down in the details. It's easy for mission creep to set in: You ask a question and get the answer; the answer raises more questions. You may be curious, but you shouldn't pursue those new questions unless they truly affect the choices you are making. Keeping due diligence moving forward rapidly and in a tight, disciplined manner is even more important than knowing everything there is to know about the business. Momentum gets deals completed, whereas a slow-paced, excessive focus on unimportant details can make them fall apart. And even if the deal does close, it is very common for the financial performance of an acquired company to decline between the LOI and closing, perhaps by as much as 2% per month, as the seller gets distracted. The longer you take, the greater the chance that the seller will become fatigued by all the questions and negotiating. Under these circumstances, another buyer can jump in, or your investors might start working on other matters and become hard to reengage. Instead, stay focused on findings that would kill, change, or confirm the deal.

Next Steps

As you complete the bulk of your confirmatory due diligence, you will begin to simultaneously focus on other acquisition-related activities: borrowing money from lenders, raising equity from an investor group, and drafting and negotiating the purchase agreement. In the next three chapters, we discuss each of these activities.

CHAPTER 18

Raising Debt

Buyers typically pay for their acquisition of a smaller firm by borrowing about two-thirds of the purchase price. As you learned earlier, some of that debt may be in the form of seller financing that you specified in your LOI. The remainder of the debt will come from a bank, in the form of either a commercial loan or a loan backed by the Small Business Administration (in the United States; other countries have different programs to foster lending to smaller firms), or from a nonbank lender.

As described in chapter 15, "Deal Terms," you will be looking primarily for a senior loan, which stands first in line to be paid, ahead of other creditors and equity holders. Senior loans are typically limited to 30% to 50% of the total value of the business, a percentage that gives the lender a large cushion of safety. Seller debt is typically 20% to 25% of the total value, and as mentioned earlier, the two types of debt usually constitute about two-thirds of the purchase price, so the sources of capital for your acquisition might look like those shown in table 18-1.

TABLE 18-1

Sources of capital for the acquisition of a small business

Senior loan	40%
Seller debt	25%
Equity	35%
Total	100%

Looking for a Senior Lender

Your search for a lender should begin when you sign the letter of intent and begin your confirmatory due diligence. Local and regional banks are a good source of senior loans, as are nonbank lenders. To find a lender for your acquisition financing, you will need to contact several institutions—perhaps dozens. Sometimes, one lender will have had a bad experience lending to a business in your company's industry and not be interested, while a different bank has had favorable results and feels comfortable with this type of business.

If your acquisition target has an existing lender relationship, start there since that bank is already familiar with the business. Otherwise, begin by approaching an SBA lender to see if you qualify for one of these attractive funding options (see the sidebar "Small Business Administration Loans"). If, on the other hand, you need to approach other banks for a conventional (non-SBA) loan, ask them three questions to identify early on whether they are likely candidates to fund your acquisition:

- **What is their preferred loan size range?** Lenders generally have a preference, and you want to deal with a lender for which your loan size is attractive and routine.

- **What is their experience and expertise in your industry?** Your application will proceed much quicker if the bank feels knowledgeable about your business. You will also be selecting a banker as well as a bank; ask your banker about their track record for getting loans approved by the institution's internal credit committee.

- **Are they an asset-based or cash-flow lender?** There are two basic types of senior lenders: asset-based or cash flow (described below). Identify which is the most appropriate for your business, and target lenders that offer that type of loan.

SMALL BUSINESS ADMINISTRATION LOANS

Before you pursue other loans, contact a local bank that advertises itself as participating in the SBA 7(a) Loan Program to determine if you qualify. We mentioned in chapter 15 that we think SBA loans are a great choice, if you qualify. These are 10-year cash-flow loans with no promises to the lender other than paying the required interest and amortization payments. They are also relatively inexpensive. You can borrow up to 80% of the acquisition cost of qualifying small businesses, up to a maximum loan size of $5.0 million.

Asset-based loans

Asset-based lending is the most common and traditional form of senior lending. Lenders of asset-based loans expect the cash flow of your company to regularly pay the interest and repay the principal on their loan over time. But if the company's cash flow declines and is no longer adequate to service the loan, these lenders have a lien on assets (such as accounts receivable, inventory, or even real estate) that will be sold to repay their loan. Typical lending ratios for asset-based lenders are 70% to 90% of current accounts receivable, plus 50% of inventory value.[1] Asset-based loans are usually less expensive than cash-flow loans and thus are preferable—if they fit the business.

Service businesses, for example, generally don't have sufficient assets to raise much debt from asset-based lenders. For example, Vector Disease Control International, acquired by Jason Pananos and Jay Davis for $6.7 million, is an extermination service business with very few tangible assets: no inventory, accounts receivable at a modest $140,000 at acquisition, and equipment so specialized that it has little resale value. Asset-based loans were not suitable for the transaction; Jason and Jay used a cash-flow lender instead.

Cash-flow lenders

Cash-flow lenders make loans to businesses that have stable, predictable profits but lack tangible assets. These lenders rely entirely on the business's future profitability as the basis of their repayment. Like asset-based lenders, cash-flow lenders lend no more than 30% to 50% of the total value of the company to create a safety cushion for their loan.

SBA-backed loans are cash-flow loans. Sometimes, local commercial banks are willing to provide cash-flow loans as well, but most often, you need to approach non-bank lenders for these types of loans. Again except for SBA-backed loans, cash-flow lenders generally charge higher interest rates than do asset-based lenders. If the loan is from a local commercial bank, the difference isn't likely to be substantial; if it is from a nonbank lender, the rate could be twice the bank rate or more.

Senior Loan Terms

Whether senior loans are based on assets or cash flow, they are codified in detailed legal documents that you will negotiate using your attorney. There are five major items to be negotiated: loan size, covenants, repayment schedule, personal guarantees, and rates and fees. Each of these items is important, but it helps to prioritize them in your negotiations. Your most important objective is to obtain the funds to make your acquisition, so the availability of a sufficiently large loan is vital. Second, you should structure the loan covenants and other restrictions to minimize the chances of default. Your third priority should be the amortization schedule: Pushing the repayments to later in the life of the loan will give you much valuable flexibility early on. Next come personal guarantees, and the final priority is rates and fees.

Rates and fees are last on our list because you should focus on getting enough debt to buy the business and to then operate it efficiently. Having debt is much more important than having *cheap* debt. Agreeing on an achievable amortization schedule and loan covenants is of paramount importance because you don't want a bump in your business's performance to result in a sudden crisis with your lender. Most businesses experience reversals along the way—you want to negotiate debt that gives you time to fix these normal problems.

Loan size

Before you apply to lenders for a specific loan amount, you will need to take several analytical steps to decide on the right amount. First, the loan needs to be large enough so that you can purchase the company: The loan plus the seller debt plus the equity you plan to raise must cover the cost of your acquisition and the associated transactions costs. Make sure that the amount of senior debt you are requesting is within the normal market range of 30% to 50% of the purchase price. Then plug these amounts into your financial model, and check that the business will be able to repay the debt as it is due. If the loan is too large, you'll need to reduce the amount and increase either the seller debt or the equity. The amount of seller debt was specified in the LOI, so increasing seller debt would require you to reopen negotiations with the seller. Raising equity seems simpler, but be sure that the amount is within the capacity of your investor network and that the projected returns to the equity fall within required market ranges (more on equity returns in chapter 19, "Raising Acquisition Equity"). It may take you a few iterations with your financial model for all these considerations to line up. Once you do line everything up, you're ready to ask for a senior loan.

A bank will generally offer you the largest loan amount that its internal credit committee is comfortable extending. But this isn't a science: You will find that two banks may propose significantly different loan amounts for the very same company. If that's the case, you can ask a bank to reconsider the loan amount because you have a larger proposal elsewhere.

In some instances, you may be unable to obtain a senior loan that is large enough for you to close the acquisition. This occurs, for example, when the historical financial results would not support the loan, perhaps because the business has had uneven results, like a turnaround. Another example is businesses that are growing rapidly; your price is higher because of the anticipated growth, but lenders are often unwilling to incorporate this future growth into their loan sizing. When you cannot get a sufficiently large senior loan, you'll need to revisit your proposed financial structure, perhaps getting a larger seller note or more equity. The simple fact is that without the money, you cannot buy the company. So, on rare occasions, deals fall apart because funding is unavailable.

Covenants

Almost all senior loans come with *covenants,* or specific promises you make to your lender. If you violate a covenant, the loan becomes due immediately. In most cases, if the violation is minor, the bank will provide a waiver. If it is more serious, the bank may require a fee, a higher interest rate, or a partial pay-down of the loan balance.

Finally, if the covenant breach reflects very bad financial performance, the lender may accelerate the loan and force repayment. Because a breach could have dire consequences, you want to make sure each covenant is achievable.

The most important covenants are the financial tests typically applied quarterly or annually. They generally take the form of ratios that compare your company's EBITDA with, say, the amount of debt owed to the lender. This is called a *leverage ratio*—for example, "Senior debt amount must be less than 2.5x the EBITDA." Or perhaps EBIDTA is compared with the amount of interest and principal repayments paid annually to the lender (*debt service coverage ratio*), as in "EBITDA must be at least 2x the annual debt service of the company."

Covenants are initially proposed by the lender. When you apply for your loan, the lender will request your projection of the company's future financial performance, discount your projection of future profitability by 15% to 20%, and then propose covenants at that discounted level.

Lenders like covenants that are just a little bit below the borrower's projected financial performance—in other words, promises that require you to operate within a narrower margin. Such covenants give them early notice of deteriorating financial performance and the ability to protect their loan. In contrast, as the borrower, you want covenants to give you more room to miss your projected performance so that you can avoid violations. As a borrower, you should always negotiate the covenants to ask for a bit more leeway. If the lender registers concern at your lack of confidence in your own projections on which the covenants are based, remind the lender that the purpose of a covenant isn't to test how good a forecaster you are; it's to make sure that the loan is very safe. At 2x debt service coverage, for example, the loan is perfectly safe, even if that represents a considerable discount from your financial projection.

The ratios also can change over time. Generally, early in the loan, your company's profitability should be able to drop at least 15% to 25% before hitting a covenant. The covenants naturally become looser in future years because the repayments you've already made have rendered the remaining loan balance increasingly secure. For example, on the day you close your loan, your actual leverage ratio might be 2.5x, while the covenant is using a ratio of 3x (table 18-2). Two years later, your EBITDA has grown to $1.5 million and you have repaid $700,000 of the loan amount, creating more "room" relative to your 3x leverage covenant (table 18-3).

Your financial model is a useful tool in helping you negotiate loan covenants. Insert the proposed covenants into your projection. Then tweak the company's performance until you hit a covenant. This will enable

TABLE 18-2

Example of a leverage ratio at closing for the acquisition of a small business

Senior loan amount	$3.0 million
EBITDA*	$1.2 million
Senior debt/EBITDA ratio	2.5x

*EBITDA, earnings before interest, taxes, depreciation, and amortization.

TABLE 18-3

Example of a leverage ratio two years after closing on an acquisition for a small business

Senior loan amount	$2.3 million
EBITDA*	$1.5 million
Senior debt/EBITDA ratio	1.5x

*EBITDA, earnings before interest, taxes, depreciation, and amortization.

you to identify which are the governing covenants—the tightest ones—and how much operating flexibility is available to you before you actually break a covenant.

Repayment schedule

Most banks (outside of the SBA loan program) try to keep the term of their loans to smaller firms to five years or less to limit the banks' risk. They will propose a repayment schedule, referred to as a *loan amortization schedule,* which will detail how the loan will be partially repaid each year during the term. Amortization schedules do not have to be level during the life of the loan; nor do they have to fully amortize the loan. It's a good idea to try to negotiate smaller amortization payments in the early years of the loan; if your business generates lots of cash, you can always prepay some of the loan. On the other hand, if there is a stumble early on, it is helpful to have the flexibility that comes from low required debt repayments. Insert the bank's proposed amortization schedule into your financial projections, and make sure enough cash is left over for setbacks in financial performance as well as for funding growth needs.

Banks will also often request an *excess cash flow sweep*: At the end of each year, if the company has generated cash after paying all operating expenses, interest expense, tax distributions, capital expenditures or other investments, and scheduled debt repayment, then a portion—usually half—of that excess cash is swept to the bank as a loan principal prepayment. Usually these prepayments are credited against the last scheduled amortization payments, so that your required repayments are not reduced until you get near the end of the loan life.

Personal guarantees

Personal guarantees by the buyer—you—to the senior lender are a common feature of loans to smaller firms. All SBA-guaranteed loans require a personal guarantee. A conventional lender will often require a personal guarantee if you own the majority of equity in the company, but the lender is likely to exempt you if investors own the majority. Signing a personal guarantee is always a matter for thoughtful consideration, as it exposes all of your own financial assets to the risk of business failure.

Rates and fees

Banks will charge you for loans in two ways. First is an interest rate on the outstanding balance. This interest rate is composed of a *base rate,* which is based on a publicly known standard market rate and which varies from month to month, and a *spread,* which is a fixed amount above that base rate.

Lenders to smaller firms also charge an array of fees in addition to the interest rate. These come under a wide range of names—due-diligence fee, commitment fee, closing fee, availability fee, or monitoring fee. Pay less attention to the names than the total amount; when receiving a proposal from a bank, you should confirm that the proposal shows all its fees and the basis by which each fee is calculated. In addition to the fees outlined, you will be required to reimburse the bank's legal fees and any other third-party expenses incurred in closing the loan.

Other terms

Most senior loans also restrict how a company's remaining cash flow can be distributed after paying senior loan service. Typically, the senior lender prohibits cash from being paid to equity owners, other than as tax distributions, while the senior loan remains outstanding.[2] If there is also a seller note financing your acquisition, the senior lender generally allows interest payments to be made as long as the senior loan is in covenant compliance, but the senior lender restricts principal pay-down on the seller note until the senior loan is repaid. The senior lender's goal is for the company's cash flow to first repay the senior loan before going to subordinate creditors or equity holders.

Negotiating and closing a bank loan is time-consuming and can take two months from the time you first identify a bank interested in lending to your company. When a bank does offer to lend you money, it will issue a formal term sheet. This is always a nonbinding document, but it outlines in detail the terms of the proposed loan. Because the document is also a starting point for negotiations, banks usually leave themselves a bit of flexibility to be responsive. When you accept a term sheet, you commit yourself to paying the bank's due-diligence and legal expenses required to close the loan; the bank then begins preparing a loan agreement and completing its own confirmatory due diligence on your company. You will be meeting the bank's due-diligence requests (with information you obtained from the seller) and, with your lawyer, negotiating the final loan document. Everybody will be working to get this done at the same time that the purchase agreement between you and the seller is completed.

Seller Debt

Seller debt takes the form of a promissory note from the company to the seller. The amount of seller debt is typically 20% to 25% of the total purchase price, the term of the note four to five years, and the interest rate 5% to 8% and usually fixed. There are rarely personal guarantees associated with seller debt.

You will negotiate several issues directly with the seller. Most obvious are note amount, term, and interest rate. In addition, there are two protective provisions that the seller may request: If you refinance the senior debt while the seller note is still outstanding, you cannot increase the amount of the new senior loan above the amount of the old one. A typical compromise is that you can increase the amount of the senior loan, but if you do, half the increase must be used to prepay the seller debt. A second request may be that no cash distributions are made to equity owners (other than tax distributions) until the seller note is fully repaid. This reasonable request should be accommodated, although we are surprised at how often sellers fail to ask for this provision.

One important evolution in the deal since you submitted your LOI (where you may have introduced the idea of seller debt into the deal) is that your senior lender's loan documents will require that the seller note be subordinate to the senior loan. This agreement allows the senior lender to block payments to the seller debt holder if the company has defaulted on the senior note. This agreement is negotiated between the bank and the seller's lawyer. Some sellers, especially those selling for the first time, are surprised and resist this provision, but in the end, the bank will insist, and the seller, eager to complete the transaction, will agree. Often, however, the cost of the agreement is that the equity investors agree to delay any payouts until the seller note is paid back.

The seller note will be drafted by your lawyer, and the subordination agreement will be drawn up by the bank lawyer. These documents will join others to be executed on closing day.

Next Steps

You've been working toward raising the debt financing for your acquisition and made progress defining the type of loan you are looking for and have begun discussions with potential lenders. The next step is to raise the equity financing; chapter 19, "Raising Acquisition Equity," leads you through that process.

NOTES

1. When receivables become past due, they are typically excluded from the borrowing base calculation by the bank. The loan-to-value percentage for inventory can vary significantly. If the inventory value is easily determined and the inventory can be sold quickly—for

example, an inventory of crude oil—the lending ratio might be 90%. If the inventory is difficult to value or hard to sell, the ratio will be lower.

2. Since the income tax obligation of your company flows through to your shareholders, you will probably distribute cash to your shareholders each year to reimburse them for the income tax payments they are obligated to make on their share of the company's pretax income. Lenders always permit this type of distribution to equity owners.

CHAPTER 19

Raising Acquisition Equity

If your prospect is a good acquisition opportunity, you should be able to quickly raise the equity you need to complete the transaction. If you have never raised a million or more dollars of equity before, this statement probably seems surprising, but it's true; there are many more people trying to invest capital than there are good investments. It's hard for most high-net-worth investors—the owner of a successful midsize business, a partner in a large law firm, and so forth—to gain access to private-equity investments. That means there are investors interested in providing equity to fund about one-third of your total purchase price—as long as the promised payoffs are high enough to reward them for the risks and illiquidity inherent in that type of investment. In our experience, the payoffs need to provide investors with at least an annual rate of return around 25%.

When you began your search, you started to assemble a group of wealthy investors who might be interested in providing equity capital to fund your acquisition. Those include the investors from your search fund and—whether your search was investor-funded or self-funded—a network of individuals you've been building up since the search phase. If you are a funded searcher, you can probably obtain most of your acquisition capital from the same group that funded your search. For the remaining equity you need, reach out to additional investors, perhaps, for example, some who were unwilling to fund the search but were interested in backing you in an acquisition. If you are a self-funded searcher, you'll need to raise all of the equity from the potential investors you've been keeping informed throughout your search.

The process for raising capital for your purchase is very similar to that outlined for raising capital for the search itself in chapter 5, "Paying for Your Search." You begin with people you know, and then you grow your network along the way. But instead of having to share stories about potential companies, you can now tell investors in concrete terms why you think your prospect is a great acquisition.

Assembling the Investment Memorandum

The *investment memorandum,* a detailed packet of information about your target company, should be sent to potential investors. Start putting this memo together once you have a signed LOI. The memo should include the following information:

☐ Information about the business and its industry. What's in the confidential information memorandum (CIM) is fine.

☐ Details on the due diligence that you've done, covering your own preliminary and confirmatory due diligence together with input from your accountant and lawyer. Give special attention to any issues that concerned you and that you resolved so that investors can get comfortable both with the specific issue and with the scope and care of your due diligence.

☐ Your financial projections.

☐ The deal terms that you are proposing to potential investors. Include the types of securities available (more on this below), the sequence of payouts, an agreement about how the company will be governed, and the amount of equity you plan to retain.

If you took funding for your search, you'll have outlined many of the deal terms for equity investors then and you'll have little flexibility on terms at this stage. If you funded your own search, you'll have more flexibility.

Types of securities

Most equity investors in smaller private companies receive a preferred stock security that provides for a return of capital plus a preferred return to investors, followed by an equity interest in the company. If, for example, you raised $3.0 million from investors, the company would repay the $3.0 million invested plus a preferred return of, say, 8%, as cash becomes available from the business and as the required debt payments are met. Once the $3.0 million plus the preferred return is paid to investors, subsequent available cash flows are divided between you and the investors. Sometimes, there is a *catch-up* to the entrepreneur so that you receive your proportional interest of the preferred return before the cash flows are divided between you and the investors.

Variations from deal to deal reflect the trade-offs entrepreneurs and investors make as they fit together their individual goals. Ari Medoff negotiated that his investors receive a high preferred return and he waived a catch-up; in return, he received a very large share of the remaining profits. Jude Tuma negotiated a more standard share of remaining profits and no catch-up to himself; in return, he benefited from a low preferred return rate to his investors.

Deal terms

If you raised money from investors to fund your search, the terms of your acquisition were set when you took the search capital. Table 19-1 returns to the acquisition model for Zeswitz Music, the company that rents musical instruments to students. We looked at that model in chapter 13, "Preliminary Due Diligence," as an example of forecasting results and to help gauge a reasonable offer price. We also learned in chapter 17, "Confirmatory Due Diligence," that Randy Shayler discovered that Zeswitz's EBITDA was 20% less than what was reported in the CIM and that he was able to negotiate a proportionally

TABLE 19-1

Zeswitz Music acquisition financial model, version 4, with search fund investors' equity

KEY ASSUMPTIONS			HYPOTHETICAL ACQUISITION FUNDING			
			Uses		**Sources**	
Purchase price as a multiple of 2012 EBITDA less 20% ($1,228)*	4		Purchase price	4,912	Bank debt	1,519
Leverage ratio, bank	30%		Acquisition costs	150	Seller debt	1,519
Debt rate, bank	6%					
Leverage ratio, seller	30%				Investor equity	2,024
Debt rate, seller	8%					
Preferred return on equity	7%			5,062		5,062
Manager's carry	25%					

YEAR ENDING DECEMBER 31

	2013	2014	2015	2016	2017
Free cash flow from table 13-3	763	801	841	883	928
50% of capital expenditures	272	286	300	315	331
Less: 20% reduction in EBITDA (due-diligence result)	262	275	288	303	318
	773	812	853	895	941
Exit (4 x 2017 EBITDA of $1,590 from table 13-3 less 20%)					5,088
Bank debt					
Beginning debt	1,519	959	327	0	0
Interest on debt	91	58	20	0	0
Debt repayment	560	632	327	0	0
Ending debt	959	327	0	0	0
Seller debt					
Beginning debt	1,519	1,519	1,519	1,135	331
Interest on debt	122	122	122	91	27
Debt repayment	0	0	384	804	331
Ending debt	1,519	1,519	1,135	331	0
Available equity cash flow after debt payments	0	0	0	0	5,670
Investors' equity					
Beginning LP (limited partnership)	2,024	2,166	2,318	2,480	2,654
Preference	142	152	162	174	186
	2,166	2,318	2,480	2,654	2,840
Capital distribution to investors	0	0	0	0	2,840
Ending LP equity	2,166	2,318	2,480	2,654	0

(continued)

TABLE 19-1 (CONTINUED)

	YEAR ENDING DECEMBER 31				
	2013	2014	2015	2016	2017
Available equity after debt and capital distributions	o	o	o	o	2,830
Manager's carry	o	o	o	o	708
Investors' carry	o	o	o	o	2,123
Investors' cash flows	o	o	o	o	4,963
Investors' internal rate of return	20%				

Note: Unless marked as a percentage or a multiple for the purchase price, all numbers are in thousands of dollars.

*EBITDA, earnings before interest, taxes, depreciation, and amortization.

lower acquisition price. In table 19-1, we've started with the assumptions of table 13-3, reduced the purchase price and exit value by 20% for the lower EBITDA, and adjusted the cash flows for the lower results. We've also added in the calculations of the equity internal rate of return. The model is structured around typical search fund terms with the searcher getting 25% of the cash flow after the equity investors received payments that equaled their investment plus a preferred rate of return of 7% in the example. The internal rate of return (IRR) is 20%, below the 25% that investors demand. This deal might be hard to fund. The search-fund investors could choose not to invest, and that might well be the end of the deal.

If the confirmatory due diligence and better understanding of the business made the future of the company look better, perhaps even great, with high financial rewards relative to the purchase price—perhaps with an annual rate of return well above 25%—then most of those benefits go to the investors who funded your search. You'll benefit from your fixed-percentage ownership of a better business, but you cannot get a higher percentage of ownership just because you found an amazing opportunity. Imagine that Randy became convinced that the lower operating expenses and capital expenditures in 2012 were sustainable. The resulting model is in table 19-2. The investors would be pleased with the 29% IRR, but Randy's share would continue to be 25% of the profits after the investors' investment and a preferred return was paid to the investors.

If you self-funded your search, you determine the terms of the equity you'll offer to investors now that you know the prospect and its attractiveness; the better the prospect, the better the deal you'll be able to structure for yourself. This flexibility is the primary benefit to self-funding your search.

To develop a plan for dividing up profits, return to the financial model you have created for your acquisition. You initially built the financial projections during your preliminary due diligence, refining them during your confirmatory due diligence. Now that you've spoken with potential lenders and have a sense of the debt available, you should complete your plan by designing the potential terms of an equity investment. Investors generally want an annual return of at least 25% on private-equity investments in a solid, profitable, smaller business. But how much of the company does that mean investors should own? To answer this question, plug some standard investor ownership terms into your financial model, and

TABLE 19-2

Zeswitz Music acquisition financial model, version 5, with search fund investors' equity with 2012 operating expenses and half of historical capital expenditures

KEY ASSUMPTIONS		HYPOTHETICAL ACQUISITION FUNDING			
		Uses		**Sources**	
Purchase price as a multiple of 2012 EBITDA less 20% ($1,228)*	4	Purchase price	4,912	Bank debt	1,519
Leverage ratio, bank	30%	Acquisition costs	150	Seller debt	1,519
Debt rate, bank	6%			Investor equity	2,024
Leverage ratio, seller	30%				
Debt rate, seller	8%				
Preferred return on equity	7%		5,062		5,062
Manager's carry	25%				

YEAR ENDING DECEMBER 31

	2013	2014	2015	2016	2017
Free cash flow assuming 2012 operating expenses and half of historical capital expenditures	1,363	1,431	1,503	1,578	1,657
Less: 20% reduction in EBITDA (due-diligence result)	316	332	349	366	384
Exit (4 x recalculated 2017 EBITDA of $1,920 less 20% = $1,537)					6,148
Bank debt					
Beginning debt	1,519	685	0	0	0
Interest on debt	91	41	0	0	0
Debt repayment	834	685	0	0	0
Ending debt	685	0	0	0	0
Seller debt					
Beginning debt	1,519	1,519	1,268	215	0
Interest on debt	122	122	101	17	0
Debt repayment	0	251	1,053	215	0
Ending debt	1,519	1,268	215	0	0
Available equity cash flow after debt payments	**0**	**0**	**0**	**980**	**7,421**
Investors' equity					
Beginning LP (limited partnership)	2,024	2,166	2,318	2,480	1,674
Preference	142	152	162	174	117
	2,166	2,318	2,480	2,654	1,791
Capital distribution to investors	0	0	0	980	1,791
Ending LP equity	2,166	2,318	2,480	1,674	0

Available equity after debt and capital distributions	o	o	o	o	5,630
Manager's carry	o	o	o	o	1,408
Investors' carry	o	o	o	o	4,222
Investors' cash flows	o	o	o	980	6,013
Investors' internal rate of return	**29%**				

Note: Unless marked as a percentage or a multiple for the purchase price, all numbers are in thousands of dollars.
*EBITDA, earnings before interest, taxes, depreciation, and amortization.

---

examine the resulting projected returns to investors. For example, start with a payout sequence like this:

1. The investors get back all their capital.

2. They then receive a 7% annual return on their invested capital (the preferred return).

3. Then you receive 25% of the amount paid to the investors as the preferred return (the catch-up).

4. Then the remaining profits are divided 75/25.

Review what level of return this deal provides to investors. If it is much above 25%, increase your ownership to move projected investor returns to about 25%. It's an iterative process to find your way to a proposed deal.

Table 19-3 shows the same model as table 19-2 except that we assume that Randy's search was self-funded. He can now increase his percentage ownership above 25% and still offer investors a return well above 25%. For example, if he kept 45% of the profits after the return of

TABLE 19-3

Zeswitz Music acquisition financial model, version 6, assuming a self-funded search with 2012 operating expenses and half of historical capital expenditures

KEY ASSUMPTIONS		HYPOTHETICAL ACQUISITION FUNDING			
		Uses		**Sources**	
Purchase price as a multiple of 2012 EBITDA less 20% ($1,228)*	4	Purchase price	4,912	Bank debt	1,519
Leverage ratio, bank	30%	Acquisition costs	150	Seller debt	1,519
Debt rate, bank	6%			Investor equity	2,024
Leverage ratio, seller	30%				
Debt rate, seller	8%				
Preferred return on equity	7%		5,062		5,062
Manager's carry	45%				

YEAR ENDING DECEMBER 31

	2013	2014	2015	2016	2017
Free cash flow assuming 2012 operating expenses and half of historical capital expenditures	1,363	1,431	1,503	1,578	1,657
Less 20% reduction in EBITDA (due-diligence result)	316	332	349	366	384
Exit (4 x recalculated 2017 EBITDA of $1,922 less 20% = $1,537)					6,148
Bank debt					
Beginning debt	1,519	685	0	0	0
Interest on debt	91	41	0	0	0
Debt repayment	834	685	0	0	0
Ending debt	685	0	0	0	0
Seller debt					
Beginning debt	1,519	1,519	1,268	215	0
Interest on debt	122	122	101	17	0
Debt repayment	0	251	1,053	215	0
Ending debt	1,519	1,268	215	0	0
Available equity cash flow after debt payments	0	0	0	980	7,421
Investors' equity					
Beginning LP (limited partnership)	2,024	2,166	2,318	2,480	1,674
Preference	142	152	162	174	117
	2,166	2,318	2,480	2,654	1,791
Capital distribution to investors	0	0	0	980	1,791
Ending LP equity	2,166	2,318	2,480	1,674	0

Available equity after debt and capital distributions	o	o	o	o	5,630
Manager's carry	o	o	o	o	2,534
Investors' carry	o	o	o	o	3,096
Investors' cash flows	o	o	o	980	4,887
Investors' internal rate of return	25%				

Note: Unless marked as a percentage or a multiple for the purchase price, all numbers are in thousands of dollars.

*EBITDA, earnings before interest, taxes, depreciation, and amortization.

the investment and payment of the preferred return, the investors' IRR would still be 25%.

One caution: It is tempting to return to your forecasts of the business and add a bit of optimism to your projections at this point, increasing the cash flows to the business and resulting in a quicker debt pay-down and significantly higher investor returns. But you will need to include your financial model in your investment memo (many investors will also ask for an electronic version), and investors will almost immediately question aggressive assumptions. Substantial growth in revenues or margin expansion are tell tale signs of over-optimism, and our experience is this too-sunny outlook will cause investors to pass on the investment. It is better to present a conservative model that delivers good returns and then tell investors why you think it may be even better. If, for example, Randy sent along the model in table 19-3, he would need to have a very convincing explanation of his two important assumptions about the substantially lower operating expenses and capital expenditures.

Approaching Investors

Once you have your investment memorandum in place, complete with proposed terms, reach out to your potential investors via email to schedule a phone conversation. Send in advance a very short description of your target company.

If the call suggests that the investor might be interested in your proposal, send the full investment memo and schedule a time to follow up again with another call to answer any questions the investor might have.

Potential investors will have numerous questions about your due diligence, the business, the securities, and so on. These meetings are important sales calls; they are not informal conversations. As with your earlier pitch for search funding, you should prepare thoroughly and stay focused on delivering your pitch in the call. Everything about your acquisition opportunity, your own preparedness, and your manner is being evaluated.

As you close in on a set of interested investors, you will need to get verbal commitments from them. We recommend soliciting more equity commitments than you need to avoid any last-minute scrambling if an investor ultimately backs out. Once you have your equity investors in hand and have agreed on the terms of their investment, your lawyer will prepare and circulate a shareholder agreement to your equity investors. In this agreement, they commit to funding their part of the acquisition.

Next Steps

You are now moving toward your acquisition on three separate fronts: you are completing your confirmatory due diligence, working with your lender to complete *their* due diligence and negotiate a loan agreement, and finalizing the shareholders' agreement with your equity investors. The last step in the process before closing is completing the purchase agreement, and that is the topic of our next chapter.

CHAPTER 20

Negotiating the Purchase Agreement

As due diligence progresses along with your confidence that this deal will close, you and your attorney need to start drafting an *asset purchase agreement,* which is the definitive legal acquisition contract. Because this is a meaningful investment of professional fees and time, you should usually wait to begin drafting the contract until after the most important confirmatory due-diligence work is satisfactorily completed.

Your attorney always creates the initial draft of the purchase agreement, and then the seller's attorney returns a marked-up copy containing their comments. That begins a negotiation between you and the seller as the two of you decide on the precise contours of the business deal. For you, the confirmatory due diligence you have conducted links seamlessly to the preparation of the purchase agreement. The schedules that are appended to the purchase agreement—third-party contracts, financial statements, employee payroll, pending litigation, physical assets, and others—represent documents that you have previously received and reviewed. You have already identified the form of the acquisition and the net working capital target. But for the seller, the preparation of the required schedules takes a lot of time and is a new and often tedious task. And if the schedules include items that you have not reviewed, you'll need to do due diligence on them. It generally it takes about a month to complete a purchase agreement.

This chapter outlines the most critical items you will need to determine as you draft the purchase agreement. Let's examine them one by one.

Your Acquisition Entity

You need to legally create a company to be the acquirer of the business you are buying. You can use the search fund company that you created as you were starting to look for an acquisition, or you can create a new acquisition entity. Because the decision is largely determined by legal considerations, your attorney will advise you on which company structure is best, given your situation. This acquisition company will also be the borrower if you are using bank debt or seller debt in the acquisition, and it will issue securities to investors if you are raising equity capital. The creation of a company will establish limited liability, meaning that your personal assets are safe from creditors looking to be paid by your company other than any personal guarantees you explicitly granted to, for example, the senior lender. It also creates only a single level of income tax on its earnings. In the United States, there are three entity forms that accomplish both of these goals: limited liability companies (LLCs), limited partnerships (LPs), and S-corporations. Today, the most commonly used entity form is the LLC because of the ease with which it can be formed and its flexibility in accommodating different deal structures for investor equity.

The Structure of Your Purchase

You decided whether the purchase transaction would be an acquisition of assets or stock when you created your LOI. Now you'll capture that decision in the purchase agreement.

You'll also want to take other steps that affect how (and how much!) you will be taxed. In the United States, if you are acquiring the stock of an LLC, LP, or S-corporation or are directly buying the assets from any of these types of entities, you should structure the purchase agreement so that you "step up" the tax basis to the price you are paying. Doing so will create valuable tax deductions under your future ownership. While the actual appraisal and valuation happens after closing, you will want to negotiate the outline of the appraisal in advance, when you are drafting the purchase agreement. As a practical matter, this means that every year for the next 15 years, the income tax liability is reduced by a deduction of at least 1/15th of the purchase price from the company's taxable income, and this deduction is passed through to you and your investors' personal tax returns.

Once you have closed on the company, you will hire an independent appraiser to allocate the purchase price to the business's tangible assets and any remaining value to goodwill. This appraisal and valuation will form the basis for future depreciation and amortization tax deductions, which can be quite significant. Buyers generally prefer that as much value as possible be allocated to tangible assets because their value depreciates more rapidly than does that of goodwill.

Although sellers frequently leave the postsale appraisal entirely to the buyer, the allocation of price can affect them because different tax rates apply to different types of assets. It is in the seller's interest to allocate the sale price to assets that carry a lower tax rate. This is why it is a good idea to negotiate the terms of the appraisal in advance.

While most smaller firms in the United States are organized as pass-through entities, if the seller organized their company as a C-corporation, you will probably not be able to effect a step-up, because the tax consequences to the seller are so unattractive that your purchase would no longer work for them. If the prospect is a C-corporation, you and your accountant, and perhaps your lawyer, will have hopefully caught this entity form as part of your due diligence, before you reach agreement on the major terms of the acquisition, including purchase price.

Representations and Warranties

Your lawyer will ask the seller to make a number of representations and warranties in the purchase agreement. These have two principal purposes: First, they provide disclosure for you. If the seller is representing that there is no litigation involving the company "other than as presented on Schedule A," then Schedule A provides you with valuable information about the company you are acquiring. Second, these representations and warranties give you the opportunity to make claims against the seller. If the seller represented that his or her company faced no litigation and you later discover undisclosed litigation, you have the opportunity to make a claim against the seller.

Buyers and sellers regularly negotiate these representations and warranties. The negotiations often occur around a so-called knowledge standard. Sellers prefer their representations to read more narrowly: "To the best of seller's knowledge, the company has all necessary permits." On the other hand, buyers want a broader representation: "Seller represents that the company has all necessary permits."

Escrows and Setoffs

A portion of the transaction proceeds are typically held back from the seller and placed in an escrow account. In smaller firm acquisitions, the size of the *cash* escrow is typically small (or sometimes zero), and instead the seller provides the buyer a right to *set off* claims against the value of the seller note or against future earn-out payments.

If you later have claims, this account will be your primary source of proceeds so that you don't have to be concerned about the ongoing creditworthiness of the seller. In addition, a holdback escrow encourages faster resolution of claims because the seller does not receive back money from the escrow until the claims are resolved. This creates a more buyer-friendly dynamic than if the sellers receive all their cash and therefore have an incentive to delay resolving claims and paying back money.

Escrows and setoffs are usually negotiated around four issues: size, survival period, basket size, and total dollar cap.

- **Size:** The amount of the seller's cash proceeds that will be held back in an escrow account to settle the claims, or the amount of the seller note subject to setoff for this purpose, or both.

- **Survival period:** The end date of the period during which claims can be made. After the survival period, any undisputed portion of the escrow is released to the seller and no new claims can be made. The survival period is usually at least long enough for the financial statements to be completed for the year in which the acquisition occurred.

- **Basket:** The minimum claim amount that is necessary for you to be entitled to funds from the escrow account. The basket's purpose is to eliminate disputes over very small claim amounts. As a buyer, however, you want it to be as small as possible so that you can have flexibility on the kinds of claims that come out of the escrow. On a $5.0 million acquisition, the basket might be $25,000 or $50,000. When the total claims exceed that threshold, then the escrow account pays from the first dollar of claims.

- **Cap:** Represented as a percentage of the purchase price, the maximum amount that the buyer can claim back from the seller. Usually, the cap amount is equal to the escrow account or setoff amount. Sometimes, however, the seller is willing to agree to a larger indemnification cap than the size of the escrow account, particularly for certain classes of claims. Sellers almost always get some cap on their indemnification: They want to know that there is a limit to the amount of their proceeds that are subject to claims from the buyer.

While each deal is unique, typical indemnification terms are as follows:

Size of escrow account or setoff:	20–30% of purchase price
Survival period for claims:	12–18 months
Basket size:	0–1% of purchase price
Total cap on claims:	20–30% of purchase price

Seller Note

Your LOI specified the important characteristics of the seller note, and you further honed your terms of seller debt as you determined your financing, which included the amount, the interest rate, and the amortization schedule. These terms are formalized as either part of the asset purchase agreement or in a separate document drawn up by your attorney. The separate document is then negotiated much like the rest of the purchase agreement.

Net Working Capital

Your LOI also specified the amount of working capital to be delivered at closing. The purchase agreement cements this arrangement and, because working capital is subject to constant changes, specifies how variances from the target will be handled. Usually the purchase price is adjusted according to an estimate of net working capital made as of the closing day, and a final net working capital settlement is done sometime after the closing, when buyer has had an opportunity to do an inventory count and to carefully review receivables and payables. Then the seller has a chance to review the buyer's final computation of net working capital, and if there is an additional deficiency, those funds are released to the buyer from the seller's escrow account. If there is a surplus, the seller receives that amount.

Key Personnel Issues

A few specific employees are critical to the company's success. These might be the departing owner or several executives and salespeople who are staying on. At the time of your purchase, you want to make sure everyone agrees on their future roles. While employment and noncompete agreements are separate from the purchase agreement, their execution is usually a condition required in the purchase agreement and they are executed simultaneously.

Noncompete agreements

Departing owners often have strong relationships with customers, suppliers, and employees. They also have an intimate knowledge of how the company operates (for example, the prices charged to each customer or the dates that contracts renew)—information that would be valuable to any competitor. You'll want the seller to sign a noncompete agreement that has a term of three to five years from the closing date and that gives you several elements of protection:

- **Noncompetition:** The seller agrees not to compete with the company for a certain period, "competing" being carefully defined to fit your specific business situation. It might be a promise not to contact existing customers, not to manufacture or sell specific products, or not to operate any similar business within a certain geographic area. Noncompete agreements prohibit any kind of participation in competing businesses: as an investor, a manager, a board member, or a consultant.

- **Confidentiality:** The seller promises to keep confidential all of the company's proprietary information.

- **Nonsolicitation:** The seller agrees not to recruit or hire any of the company's employees.

Seller transition

Most buyers want the seller to remain with the business during a transitional period; you should negotiate the transition agreement at the same time as the purchase agreement. Typically, this arrangement includes a short period, one to three months, during which the seller continues to work full time at the company and is paid as a salaried employee. After that, there is a longer period, usually one year, when the seller makes himself or herself available on a consulting basis and receives hourly compensation.

Employment agreements

If the company you are buying has key employees who would be difficult to replace or harmful if they went to a competitor, you should discuss with them their roles going forward and potentially put in place employment agreements. You'll get the contractual protection of non-competition, confidentiality, and nonsolicitation agreements as provisions of the employment agreements, and your employees get greater clarity on their terms of employment and perhaps an enhancement to compensation such as a performance-related bonus, stock options, or a contractually guaranteed severance period.

When Randy Shayler was acquiring Zeswitz Music, he understood the value of the excellent relationships its sales force had established with school band directors. Accordingly, he signed its top salespeople to noncompete agreements as part of a set of improvements he made to the sales force commission system.

The Closing

The weeks leading up to the closing are a busy period for everyone involved in the acquisition and especially for you. As you approach the closing day, you are finalizing a set of interrelated documents discussed in this chapter:

- The purchase agreement

- Noncompetition, nonsolicitation, and confidentiality agreement with the seller

- Employment agreements with key employees

- Loan agreement with your lender

- Seller note agreement with the seller

- Stock purchase agreement between your entity and its investors (and probably an employment agreement between your entity and yourself)

Your job is to communicate constantly with the different people involved with these various documents, solving problems that emerge and moving them toward completion. It is typical for an unanticipated issue or two to arise as closing approaches, and these can surely add stress to the process. Our advice is to keep moving forward and solve each problem as it emerges. Just as you imagine the huge costs of abandoning your acquisition this late in the process, the seller also has psychologically committed to the sale and would be loath to start over. Both sides have strong incentives to work together to close the acquisition.

CHAPTER 21

The Closing Day and Beyond

The actual closing of your acquisition will be anticlimactic. The various documents are gradually assembled and reviewed by buyer's and seller's attorneys, and signature pages emailed to one of the lawyers, who holds them in escrow. Once all the pages have been collected, the wire transfers are released and you become the owner of your own firm. Congratulations!

There are a few things to keep in mind as you make the transition to ownership. And while each company will have different priorities, there are four essential tasks you should focus on right after your closing.

First, you want to introduce yourself to all your managers and employees and reassure them that they aren't going to see any immediate changes. All of them will be wondering what your new ownership means for them. And if they are spending too much time wondering, they won't be productive. This is also an opportunity to speak about your goals for the company at a general level, whatever they are: excellent service to customers, commitment to quality, new ways to grow the business, a satisfying work environment. It is also an opportunity for the staff to ask you questions and begin to build confidence in you. But don't be too specific in your plans or promises yet. You don't yet know enough about the company, and people will respect your professional maturity if you say, "I want to take some time to learn before I make a decision about that."

Second, if you have a transition arrangement with the former owner, you want to be clear both with employees and with customers how the transition will work. Your employees have developed the habit of going to the former owner with their questions and requests for approval, and they will need specific guidance on how decisions are now made. There is no one correct division of roles, but talk over the plan with the former owner, and then make a clear statement such as: "I'm delighted that Ms. Smith has agreed to a six-month transition. I will be taking over the business as of today and running it, but she will be around here as my valued advisor." Or: "Mr. Jones will continue to oversee sales and customer service while I learn that part of the business; you can come to me on any financial or production matters." The goal of these communications is to eliminate confusion over who does what after the sale and to keep everyone focused on their work.

Third, take control of the cash. The most common reason smaller firms run into trouble is that they run out of cash. The prior owner probably ran the business largely debt-free, but you will be running the same business with acquisition debt to service. To track your cash flow, set up a process whereby you approve all payments before they go out, and review your accounts-receivable balances at least weekly. Finally, you should implement a 90-day rolling cash flow forecast: Every month, you forecast cash receipts and expenditures for the upcoming three months. This practice will help you avoid cash crises by identifying early when cash will get tight so you can take actions like redoubling collections efforts, slowing payment of accounts payable, or even arranging a line of credit at a bank.

Fourth, go meet your clients. They will like meeting the boss, and you will get plenty of ideas about how to improve service and how to sell additional products. When business partners Patrick Dickinson and Michael Weiner bought Castronics, the pipe threading company in Nebraska, they interviewed every major customer. Patrick later commented: "Every single one of our new product and service ideas came from these interviews. We didn't implement every idea the customers suggested, but every idea we did implement originated in this set of interviews."

Finally, don't rush into making big decisions in the first few months. Most of these can wait. Notwithstanding your thorough due diligence, you still have much to learn about running your new company, and you will make better decisions with a few months' experience under your belt. At the same time, don't be paralyzed— you'll still need to make numerous little decisions every day. Most will be right; some will be wrong. When you figure out the wrong ones, you can go back and fix them. That's part of the beauty of being your own boss.

The weeks after closing will be exciting, busy, and filled with learning. You will be fully engaged and pulled in more directions than even an extended business day can accommodate. Don't worry; it will all settle down. If you've come this far, you are smart, energetic, and well equipped to handle the learning curve.

Conclusion: Parting Thoughts

Thousands of smaller firms are sold every year, and many people have successfully acquired an existing business that is enduringly profitable. So why not you too? As you have seen, to succeed as an entrepreneur through acquisition, you don't need a specific business idea. You don't need operating experience in an industry, and you don't need capital. It turns out that the principal barrier to becoming an acquirer is your own willingness to pursue an acquisition. Our goal in writing this book is to help you to decide if entrepreneurship through acquisition is really for you and to empower you to do it if it is. The best way to address this question is not by asking yourself, "Do I want to be an entrepreneur?," but by asking, "Do I want to do what an entrepreneur does?" Hopefully, our journey through each of the steps involved helps you to visualize the process and decide whether this extraordinary professional opportunity is right for you.

Indication of Intent (IOI) for Zeswitz Music

[VIA EMAIL]
October 23, 2012
Mr. Sharif Tanamli
Managing Director
Lenox Hill Capital Advisors, Inc.
75 Rockefeller Plaza, 17th Floor
New York, NY 10019

Dear Sharif:

Per our telephone conversations and based on the confidential information memorandum dated September 2012, this letter sets forth the non-binding preliminary indication of interest by Succession Leadership Capital, LLC ("SLC"), in acquiring Rayburn Musical Instruments Pennsylvania, LLC ("Zeswitz" or "Company").

Thank you again for bringing this opportunity to our attention. As a former music student, I thoroughly understand the vibrant role of musical education in the lives of young men and women. Furthermore, as an entrepreneur and investor, I deeply appreciate Zeswitz's capabilities and strong history of excellent service in the Pennsylvania, New Jersey, and Maryland area.

Together with you, [the Sellers], I look forward to exploring ways to keep Zeswitz in considerate and capable hands. Together, we can determine if SLC is the right buyer to deliver a bright future for Zeswitz and the young musicians and educational communities that depend on its excellent service.

For your consideration, the outline of our proposal is as follows:

- *Enterprise value:* Based on Zeswitz's projected and adjusted EBITDA for the twelve months ended December 31, 2012, of approximately $1.54 million, we would value the company at 4x EBITDA, or $6.14 million on a total enterprise debt-free, cash-free, and tax liability-free basis. Our valuation assumes that the financial condition of the Company is reasonable as presented in the Offering Memorandum dated September 2012 and that additional inventory described on page 11 of the memorandum is included in the purchase to help manage seasonal variability in rental demand. Buyer and Sellers would agree to pay for their own outside expenses relating to the transaction, including legal, banking, and advisory fees.

- *Form of consideration:* SLC would create a new company ("Newco") to purchase 100% of the stock or assets of the Company for cash and other consideration. While it is our preference to structure the transaction as a purchase of assets, we are prepared to consider a purchase of the Company's stock under a structure that would preserve the tax deductibility of goodwill.

In our contemplated structure, SLC would require Sellers to hold an earn-out note equal to $1.54 million in total.

- *Working capital:* The purchase price would be subject to the Company's having a mutually agreed-upon level of working capital at closing. The target working capital would be determined after a review of the monthly working capital balances over the last year. Working capital would be defined as current assets (excluding cash and tax-related assets) less current liabilities (excluding debt and tax-related liabilities).

- *Financing:* SLC will fund the required equity for the transaction from its own funds. We would introduce our financing sources early into the process in order to establish our capital structure. SLC may also raise senior debt sourced through customary financial institutions.

- *Timing and approvals:* We anticipate closing the transaction within 60 to 90 days of signing a letter of intent. By request of the Sellers and with full cooperation to speed the due-diligence process, SLC can make every effort to close by December 31, 2012, to avoid any new tax consequences that may arise in the new year. The decision to consummate a transaction will be made solely by SLC. There are no other outside approvals required.

- *Management:* It is the intention of SLC to retain certain employees of the Company. However, we have not had any discussions with management to determine if there would be any employees who would not be part of the transaction. A key managers' equity options plan would be put in place to allow the management team to earn additional equity interests in the form of Newco common stock.

- *Due-diligence requirements:* Our indication of interest is subject to customary operational, financial, and legal due diligence as well as reaching mutually satisfactory arrangements with the key managers of the Company and the execution of sale and purchase agreements. At the appropriate time, SLC would also perform due diligence on the Company's major customers and suppliers. To assist us during due diligence, we would expect to engage outside advisors in the areas of legal, accounting, environmental, insurance, and employee benefits.

- *Background:* The key members of SLC have significant operational, strategic, and financial experience to lead and grow the Company. We would encourage [the Sellers] to speak to our group of advisors during the engagement to understand our qualifications, backgrounds, and objectives.

- *Contact:*
  Randy M. Shayler II
  President and Managing Director
  Succession Leadership Capital, LLC
  (617) XXX-XXXX
  Randy@SuccessionLeadership.com

Thank you for your consideration. Upon your review of this letter, I look forward to hearing from you to schedule a conference call to discuss our proposal and our mutual availability for an in-person management meeting.

Sincerely yours,

Randy M. Shayler II
President and Managing Director

Letter of Intent (LOI) for Zeswitz Music

[VIA EMAIL]

December 13, 2012

[Seller's name and address]

Dear [Seller]:

The purpose of this letter (the "Letter") is to set forth certain nonbinding understandings and certain binding agreements between Succession Leadership Capital, LLC, a Delaware limited-liability company or its affiliate ("Prospective Buyer"), and [the Seller] (referred to collectively herein as "Prospective Seller") with respect to the possible acquisition of all of the outstanding capital stock of Rayburn Musical Instruments Pennsylvania, LLC (DBA "Zeswitz"), a Delaware limited-liability company (the "Company" or "Zeswitz"), which is owned beneficially and of record by the Prospective Seller, on the terms set forth below.

1. *Basic transaction:* Prospective Buyer will acquire all of the outstanding capital stock of the Company (the "Shares"), all of which are owned beneficially and of record by the Prospective Seller.

2. *Purchase price:* Subject to Prospective Buyer's further due diligence and based on Zeswitz's projected and adjusted EBITDA for the twelve months ended December 31, 2012 of approximately $1.54 million, we would value the company at 4x EBITDA, or $6.14 million, on a total enterprise debt-free, cash-free, and tax-liability-free basis. The purchase price (the "Purchase Price") will be $6,140,000, assuming that an appropriate level of working capital shall be included with the business at closing.

3. *Form of payment:*

   (a) $4,604,000 of the Purchase Price shall be paid in cash at closing.

   (b) $1,535,000 shall be paid in the form of a Note (the "Note"). The Note will bear interest at the rate of 5% per year, with interest payable annually in arrears. The principal of the Note will be paid in full at the end of its five-year term. The Note will be subordinated to senior indebtedness of the Prospective Buyer. The terms of the Note shall be subject to acceptance by the Prospective Buyer's senior lenders.

4. *Proposed escrow agreement:* After the closing, the Prospective Buyer and Prospective Seller would enter into an agreement that would contain provisions to adjust the principal of the Note described in 3(b) above to secure the Prospective Buyer against and undisclosed liabilities, misrepresentations, and

breaches of warranties, covenants, and agreements by the Prospective Seller.

5. *Purchase agreement and closing date:* The Prospective Buyer and the Prospective Seller shall seek to negotiate a definitive purchase agreement (the "Purchase Agreement") with the intention of closing the transaction by March 1, 2013.

6. *Conditions:* The closing of the transactions contemplated hereby shall be subject to fulfillment, among other things, of the following conditions:

    (a) Completion of a due-diligence review by the Prospective Buyer of the Seller and its business, affairs, condition (financial, commercial, legal, and otherwise) and prospects, and any related matters, the results of which are satisfactory in the sole discretion of the Prospective Buyer.

    (b) Execution of a Purchase Agreement that is satisfactory to the Prospective Buyer and includes standard warranties with respect to the business and financial condition of the Company.

    (c) The Prospective Buyer shall have entered into a noncompetition agreement with [the Seller] satisfactory to Prospective Buyer.

    (d) The Prospective Seller shall have operated the Company until the closing in the ordinary course and consistent with prior practices, and no material adverse change shall have occurred. The Prospective Seller shall not engage in extraordinary transactions without Prospective Buyer's approval, including but not limited to:

- Disposal of assets

- Materially increasing the annual level of compensation of any employee, or increasing, terminating, amending, or otherwise modifying any plan for the benefit of employees

- Issuing any equity securities or options, warrants, rights, or convertible securities

- Paying any dividends, redeeming any securities, or otherwise causing assets of the Company to be distributed to any of its shareholders

- Borrowing any funds, under existing credit lines or otherwise

(e) All required consents of governmental authorities and other third parties shall have been obtained.

(f) The Buyer being satisfied that the Seller is in compliance with all applicable environmental laws and that its facilities are free from environmental liabilities.

7. *Expenses:* The Prospective Seller and the Buyer shall each bear the respective costs and expenses of all attorneys, accountants, and advisors retained by or representing them in connection with this transaction.

8. *Inspection and access to information:* The Prospective Seller will permit full access to, and will make available to the Prospective Buyer's representatives for inspection and review, all properties, books, records, accounts, and documents of or relating to the Company as may be reasonably requested from time

to time. The Prospective Seller will also make the employees, accountants, attorneys, and other advisors of the Company and Prospective Seller available for consultation and permit access to other third parties for confirmation of any information so obtained.

9. *Nondisclosure:* Without the prior approval of the Prospective Buyer, the Prospective Seller will not disclose or discuss this letter of intent, its existence, or its terms and conditions, to or with any persons other than their attorneys, accountants, financial advisors, and such of the Prospective Seller's executives as may be required to know the same in implementing the provisions of this letter of intent ("Insiders"). The Prospective Seller shall use best efforts to prevent the Insiders from disclosing or discussing this letter of intent, its existence, or its terms and conditions to or with any person that is not an Insider.

10. *Competing offers:* From the date of signing this exclusivity agreement until March 1, 2013 (the "Exclusive Period"), the Company, the Prospective Seller, and their representatives and agents shall not, directly or indirectly, (a) solicit any competing offers for the purchase of the Company (whether through a sale of stock, a merger, or otherwise) or its assets or (b) negotiate or otherwise respond to any unsolicited offer or indication of interest with respect to any such purchase; provided, however, the Prospective Seller shall be free to respond to other buyers by explaining the terms of this letter. If the Company, the Prospective Seller, or their representatives and agents receive any such offer or indication of interest, the Prospective Seller will immediately forward a copy to the Prospective Buyer. The Exclusive Period shall expire

unless extended by mutual agreement of the Prospective Buyer and the Prospective Seller.

11. *Early termination:* The Prospective Buyer may terminate this agreement at any time with immediate effect by providing written notice to the Prospective Seller. The Prospective Buyer must do so upon making a decision not to pursue the purchase of the Company or its assets.

By signing this letter of intent, the parties agree to be legally bound only by paragraphs 5, 7, 8, and 9. The other provisions of this letter of intent are intended as a statement of intent only, and no party shall be legally bound to proceed with the transaction contemplated hereby unless and until a definitive Purchase Agreement has been negotiated and signed by such party, and then only upon the terms and conditions set forth in such definitive Purchase Agreement.

If the foregoing terms and conditions are acceptable, so indicate by signing and dating both of the enclosed copies of this letter of intent, and then returning one to the undersigned. This letter of intent shall expire if not accepted by you by 5:00 p.m. on Friday, September 21, 2012.

Very truly yours,

Randy M. Shayler II
Managing Director
Succession Leadership Capital, LLC
cc: Sharif Tanamli, Lenox Hill Capital Advisors, Inc.

Agreed to and accepted:

_____

[The Seller]
President and CEO, Zeswitz Music

Index

Index

About the Authors

Richard S. Ruback is the Willard Prescott Smith Professor of Corporate Finance at Harvard Business School. He has taught a variety of corporate finance courses throughout his career. Over the last few years, he and Royce Yudkoff have been developing and teaching a new second-year case course, "The Financial Management of Smaller Firms," and a field course, "Entrepreneurship through Acquisition," both of which are focused on the entrepreneurial acquisition of smaller firms.

Ruback earned his PhD in business administration at the University of Rochester in 1980 and taught at the MIT Sloan School of Management before joining the HBS faculty as a visiting professor in 1987. He was appointed associate professor in 1988 and full professor in 1989. Ruback has served as an editor for the *Journal of Financial Economics* and is the author of numerous articles on corporate finance and valuation.

Ruback has served as a consultant to corporations on corporate finance issues and has acted as an independent advisor to outside directors. He also served as an expert witness on valuation and security issues.

Royce Yudkoff is a Professor of Management Practice at Harvard Business School.

Yudkoff cofounded and served for over 20 years as Managing Partner of ABRY Partners, a leading private equity investment firm. During his tenure the firm completed hundreds of acquisitions across various industries. Yudkoff also served on numerous corporate boards.

Yudkoff earned his MBA at Harvard Business School, graduating as a Baker Scholar, and his AB at Dartmouth College, graduating as a Rufus Choate Scholar.

Notes

Notes

Notes

Notes